Questions and Answers on Jainism for the Parliament of Religions held at Chicago U.S.A. in 1893.

Questions and Answers on Jainism for the Parliament of Religions held at Chicago U.S.A. in 1893.

by

LATE MAHAMUNI SHRIMAT
VIJYANANDSURI

GYAN

Published by

Gyan Publishing House
5, Ansari Road
Daryaganj, New Delhi-110002
Phone: 011-47034999, 9811692060
E-mail: books@gyanbooks.com

Distribution Network
gyanbooks.com
India, USA, Canada, UK, Australia, France

ISBN : 978-81-212-6141-8 (PB)
First Published, 1918

2nd Impression 2022

Printed at: Gyan Press, Delhi.

Questions and Answers on Jainism for the Parliament of Religions held at Chicago U.S.A. in 1893.
Author: Late Mahamuni Shrimat Vijyanandsuri

Questions and Answers on Jainism for the Parliament of Religions held at Chicago U. S. A. in 1893.

BY

LATE MAHAMUNI SHRIMAT VIJYANANDSURI.

TRANSLATED & PUBLISHED

BY

SHRI ATMANAND JAIN PUSTAK PRACHARAK
MANDAL, ROSHAN MOHALLA, AGRA.

1918.

B. CHUNNILAL PANNALAL JEWELLER, BOMBAY.

PUBLISHER'S NOTE.

This book was originally published in 1905 with an introduction in Hindi by Lala Jaswant Rai Jaini of Lahore, and although the Hindi edition has met, in an ample, measure, the needs of the Hindi knowing public interested in the religion of the Jains, it has proved but of little use to English-educated men—more especially to the people of Chicago and other places in America interested in Jainism, at whose request and for whose benefit the book was written by the distinguished author on the occasion of the World's Parliament of religions at Chicago. Moreover, there is at present a growing desire among western scholars to know more of Jainism and its tenets, and to them the Hindi edition is of little use. In order to meet these requirements and to make known to the western world the eternal truths of Jainism which occupies a high place among the ancient religions of the world, we have ventured, with the permission of the publisher of the Hindi edition, to bring out this English translation of the book and trust that it will be favorably received by the public.

We are greatly indebted to Babu Kannoo Mal M. A. for the considerable trouble he has taken in translating this book from Hindi and to Babu Chand Mal, B. A. LL.B., Agra, for the pains taken by him in correcting the proofs.

Our thanks are, in no little measure, due to Seth Chunnilal Pannalal Jeweller, Bombay, for the generious pecuniary help he has so kindly given us in bringing out this English edition of the book.

Shri Atmanand Jain Pustak Pracharak Mandal,
Roshan Mohalla, AGRA.

A short account of the life of Shrimat Vijayanandsuri-popularly known as Shri Atmaramji.

Twenty two years have gone by since the death of Shri Vijayanandsuri, the well-known Jain Sadhu of the Swetamber sect. He was born in the village of Lahara, District Ferozpur (Punjab) on the first of Chaitra Shukla in Vikram year 1893. He was a Brahma Kshattriya by caste. His father's name was Ganeshchandra and mother's, Rupdevi. He lost his father in early childhood and was brought up by his mother. He was given in charge of Seth Jodhmal of Jira (Punjab) for education in Vikram year 1903.

He studied Hindi and Arithmetic. At times he used to visit Sthanakvasi Sadhus of the place and began to study about religion. In Vikrama 1910 he was initiated as a Sthanakvasi Sadhu. His intellect was keen: he used to commit to memory 100 verses a day. He had learnt the Shastras from the Sthanakvasi Sadhus but he began to entertain doubts as regards the interpretation as given by them. Fortunately he began to study Sanskrit Grammar and other philosophical and logical works with a Pandit.

He fearlessly gave up the Sthanakvasi doctrine and came to Ahmedabad in V. year 1932. He was initiated as a Swetamber Sadhu by Buddhi-vijayji, a Jain Sadhu of the place. In the V. year 1943, he went to Palitana, Kathiawar, and stayed there for four months during the rainy season. Here he was given the title of 'Acharya' by the Sangha ; and from that time he was called by the name of Shri Vijayanandsuri.

Then he travelled on foot from Gujerat to the Punjab. During the travel he brought to light the hidden Jain Literature. The Jain Bhandars of different places of Rajputana were examined by him. He got many old important manuscripts fairly copied out.

For many years he lived in the Punjab. His fame spread through the different parts of the country. Many people of other sects came and discussed with him on matters of religion. He answered their arguments in a mild, courteous and dispassionate manner. His tone was inspiring, and the hearers were at times astonished at his pecular tact of answering the questions. His ideas were liberal. He was serene and calm of desposition.

Many questions on Jainism were put to him by Dr. A. F. Rudolf Hoernele through Maganlal Dalpatram in the Vikram year 1945. Dr. Hoernele was greatly satisfied with the answers. He wrote to Maganlal in 1888 " Please convey to the latter (Muni Maharaj) the expression of my thanks for the great trouble he has taken to reply so promptly and so fully to my questions. His answers were satisfactory." In the introduction of the Upasakdasanga, which Dr. Hornele has edited and translated he writes " For some of this information I am indebted to Muni Maharaj Atmaramji, Anandvijayji, the well-known and highly respected Sadhu of the Jain Community throughout India and author of (among others) two very useful works in Hindi."

In Vikram year 1949, he received an invitation from Chicago to attend 'the World's Parliament of Religions. On account of religious and personal restrictions he could not go, but he sent his representative, Mr. Virchand Raghavji Gandhi, B. A. to Chicago to represent Jainism at the Parliament.

He was the author of a number of works in

Hindi. The important works are as follows:—Tatwanirnaya Prâsâd (तत्त्वनिर्णयप्रासाद), Jaina Tatwâdarsha (जैनतत्त्वादर्श), Agnântimir-bhâsker (अज्ञानतिमिरभास्कर), Samayktwa Shalyodhâr (सम्यक्त्वशल्योद्धार), and Chicago-Prasnottar (चिकागो प्रश्नोत्तर).

Many Jain temples were built in the Punjab by his teaching. About 15000 persons were converted to Jainism by his strenuous efforts. Many Pathshalas and Libraries were established by him in the districts of the Punjab and in different other parts of the country.

Spending his life in doing good deeds he passed away from this world in Vikram year 1953, Jyesta Shukla 13, in Gujranwala (Punjab). The event of his death was mysterious. At midnight he got up from bed and sat in the posture of Padmâsana. He called his pupils before him and said to them 'Oh, Now I go, Arhan !'

'Lives of great men all remind us
We can make our lives sublime,
And departing leave behind us
Foot prints on the sands of time.'

(Longfellow.)

THE SHRINE OF LATE MAHAMUNI
SHRI ATMARAMJI GUJRANWALA (PUNJAB)
V. 1953.

बन्धु र्न नः स भगवानरयोऽपि नान्ये
साक्षान्न दृष्टतर एकतमोऽपि चैषाम्।
श्रुत्वा वचः सुचरितं च पृथग्विशेष
वीरं गुणातिशयलोलतया श्रिताःस्म ॥१॥
(श्री हरिभद्रसूरि)

Introduction.

The following letter was received by Shri Shri Tapagachhacharya Nyayambhonidhi Shrimat Vijayananda Suri, popularly known as Shri Atmaramji, through the Jain Association of India, Bombay.

Worlds' Congress Auxiliary
Committee on Religious Congress,
Rev. John Henry Barrows D. D.,
Chairman,
Chicago U. S. A. November 16th 1892.

2330 Michigan Ave.

Mr. Atmaramji,
Bombay,
India.

Please address me
William Pipe,
2330 Machigan Ave,
Chicago,
United States of America.

Dear Sir,

There will be mailed to you in the course of a week an appointment as a member of the Advisory Council of the Parliament of the Relegions to be held in Chicago in 1893. In the meantime the Chairman instructs me to ask you if you will kindly forward to me at your earliest convenience two photographs of yourself and a short sketch of your life. These are to be used in preparing the illustrated account of representatives of the great faiths of the world. Will you therefore give this matter your earnest consideration and forward to me as soon as possible what is requested ? Some other pictures and explanatory literature that would illustrate any feature of Hinduism would be much appreciated. With fraternal greetings,

I am,

Faithfully and sincerely yours,

William Pipe.

A reply to this letter was sent by the Jains of Bombay through Mr. Vír Chand Raghavaji Gándhi B. A., M. R. A. S., in consultation with the Muniráj Atmá Rámjí. The purport of the reply was that the Muni Mahárāj had received the letter and was highly pleased to hear of the undertaking about holding a Religious Parliament at Chicago. It was also stated that the Muni Raj regretted that owing to oldage, religious restrictions and some other private reasons he was unable to personally attend the Parliament of religions in compliance with the invitation. As desired, two photos of the Muniraj and a short biographical account of him together with some other interesting photos were also sent, an acknowledgment for which was requested.

To this letter the following reply was received.

Chicago U. S. A. April 3rd, 1893

Muni Atmaramji,
9, Bank Street Fort,
Presidency Mills Co. Ld.

Reverend Sir,

I am very much delighted to receive your acceptance of your appointment together with the photographs and the biography of your remarkable life. Is it not possible for you to attend the Parliament in person? It would give us great pleasure to meet you. At any rate, will you not be able to prepare a paper which will convey to the occidental mind, a clear account of the Jain Faith, which you so honorably represent? It will give us great pleasure and promote the ends of the Parliament if you are able to render this service.

I send you several copies of my second report. Hoping to hear from you soon and favorably, I remain with fraternal regards,

Yours cordially,
John Henry Barrows,
Chairman,
Committee on Religious Congress.

A reply to the above letter was sent through Shah Magan Lâl Dalpat Râm, acknowledging the receipt of the letter and intimating that, in compliance with the wishes expressed therein, the Muni Maharaj had undertaken to write a contribution on the Jain Faith.

The following is the reply received.

Chicago U. S. A. June 12th 1893.

My dear Sir,

I am desired by the Rev. Dr. Barrows to make an immediate acknowledgment of your favour of May 13th. It is eminently to be desired that there should be present at the Parliament of Religions, a learned representative of the Jain community.

We are indeed sorry that there is no prospect of having the Muni Atmaramji with us and trust the community over which he presides will depute some one to represent. It is, I trust, needless for me to say that your delegate will be received by us in Chicago with every distinction, and during his stay here, will receive our hospitality in as great a measure as we are able to accord it. If you therefore decide to send a representative, will you kindly cable the fact to me ? The paper which learned Muni is preparing, will indeed be very welcome and will be given a place in the programme in keeping with the high rank of its author. Although we here in Chicago are a long distance from you, the name of Muni Atmaramji is frequently alluded to in religious discussions. For the purpose of illustrating the volumes which are to record the proceedings of the Parliament of Religions I am in want of a few pictures to illustrate the rites and ceremonies of the Jain Faith. May I ask you to procure these for me (at any expense) and send at yonr earliest convenience.

I am,
Very truly yours,
WILLIAM PIPE,
Private Secretary.

This letter was passed on by Muni Atma Ramji to the Jain Association, India, with the remarks that it would be well if the Jains at Bombay were to consider the matter of sending Vir Chand Raghavji Gandhi as a representative of Jain faith to the Parliament. He added that by his deputation as a delegate to the Parliament of the religions of the world he would be able to give publicity to the religion of the Jains to all those who did not know what Jainism and its tenets were, and that the course was calculated to disseminate the truths of Jainism far and wide. This opinion of the Muniraj was accepted by the gentlemen of Bombay, because they implicitly believed in his words and were convinced that the opinion expressed by Muniraj could never be against their scripture or prejudicial to them in any way, for they well knew that in the modern times there was none equal to him in the knowledge and scholarship of Jain religious literature. Having thus considered the matter, the Jain Association of Bombay requested Mr. Vir Chand Gandhi to go as their delegate to Chicago. On this occasion at the request of Mr. Vir Chand Gandhi as well as that of Chicago committee on Religious Congress the Muniraj wrote this work in the form of questions and answers on Jainism. I venture to publish the work for the benefit of my brethren. As the book was specially written for the Chicago Parliament and contained answers to the questions received from Chicago, it was aptly entitled the "Chicago Prashnotar *i. e.*, Questions and Answers on Jainism for the Chicago Parliament of religions. The name and learning of the author of the book being universally known, it is needless for me to dilate on the merits of his books. Nor can I do justice to the task, even if I were to attempt it. How can I be considered qualified enough to do full justice to the merits of the works of an author about whom occidental scholars and savants have expressed such a high opinion ? The following is an extract in this connection from the English translation of Upasakdasâng Sutra by Dr. A. F. Rodolph Hornell, Secretary of the Asiatic Society of Bengal.

"In a third Appendix (No. III) I have put together some additional information, that I have been able to gather since publishing the several fasciculi. For some of this information,

I am indebted to Muni Maharaj Atma Ramji, Anand Vijayji, the well-known and highly respected Sadhu of the Jain community throughout India, and author of (among others) two very useful works in Hindi, the Jaina Tattvadarsha mentioned in note 276 and the Ajnana Timira Bhaskara. I was placed in communication with him through the kindness of Mr. Magan Lal Dalpat Ram. My only regret is that I had not the advantage of his invaluable assistance from the very beginning of my work. For some useful suggestions and corrections I am also indebted to Mr. Virchand R. Gandhi, the Honorary Secretary to the Jain Association of India."

On the 21st page of "The World's Parliament of Religions," published in London, there is a photo of the Muniji Maharaj bearing the following eulogy.

" No man has so peculiarly indentified himself with the interests of the Jain Community as Muni Atmaramji. He is one of the noble bands sworn from the day of initiation to the end of life to work day and night for the high mission they have undertaken. He is the High priest of the Jain community and is recognised as the highest living authority on Jain Religion and literature by Oriental scholars."

The above has also appeared at page 3 of the treatise entitled "Eulogies to holy places." Dr. Hoernell has written certain eulogistic verses in Sanskrit on Muniji in the beginning of his publication on Upasak Dasang Sutra, the translation of which is given below :—

"(1) Thou art like the sun in dispelling the black clouds of ignorance ; thou establishest the minds of others on the sea of nector of good and noble instructions ; thou cuttest asunder all knots of doubts ; thou art beyond the eighteen blemishes condemned by Jainism. Thou art unsurpassingly great in the knowledge of the spiritual lore of Jains and that thou art all-wise.

(2) For the purpose of dispelling the ignorance of all good men, thou hast written the works entitled "Agyan Timirbhaskar" and "Jain Tattvadarsha."

(3 & 4). O Master of bliss, O glorious soul, O Enjoyer of spiritual knowledge, O great sage, O unfailing answerer of all my questions ; O purified soul ! In recognition of the good thou

hast done me, I dedicate this book to thee in all sincerety of feeling as a mark of my gratitude."

The reader of the present work will find all necessary information regarding the following questions :—

What is God ? What kind of God ought to be adored ? In what way do the Jains and in what way do the followers of other religions believe in God ? Whether God can be proved as the creator of the universe or no ? What is action and how is it internally and externally classified ? What bondages are caused by what actions and what are their fruits ? What is that which leads from one state of existence to another state of existence ? What connection is there between the soul and the actions ? Does the soul perform the actions itself or is led by some other force to perfom them ? Does the soul enjoy the fruits of its actions itself or is allowed by some other to enjoy them ? In what matters do all religions agree unanimously? Has the soul the power of becoming God or no ? Does the soul return to the world after liberation or no ? Whether or not is it possible for the world being depleted of living beings when there is a continuous streams of the souls going into liberation which prevents their return ? How is the transmigration of soul established ? How is the existence of soul proved ? What advantages are there in worshiping God and loving God, and how should this adoration be made ? What form of image-worship should be observed and why ? What connection between God and man do religions believe in ? What are the duties of an ascetic and what of a house-holder ? What are the prescribed characteristics of the spiritual and the worldly life ? What is the necessity and advantage of the study of various religious books, and what are the rules regulating such a study ? Is there an incarnation of God or no ? If so, whether the liberated soul of God catches any contamination by the process of incarnation ? Has or has not God any defects ?

In addition to the above questions, the author has also discoursed on such topics as the re-purification of a contaminated soul, rules calculated to ward ofl the fear of death, the classes and characteristics of religion etc. etc.

In consideration of the subjects treated in

Mr. VEERCHAND RAGHAVJI GANDHI teaching Jain philosophy to a lady in America, 1893.

in the book it would not be inappropriate if it is entitled "Tattvapunj" or collection of cardinal truths.

This work after completion was handed over to Mr. Vir Chandra Gandhi, who by its aid created a thirst in the minds of the people at Chicago and other places for spiritual knowledge to such an extent that he was again invited to America. The invitation was gladly accepted by Mr. Vir Chundra Gandhi who resolved to go there with his family. On the occasion of his departure, the spiritual-minded Jains of Bombay presented several addresses to him. For fear of space, the purport of only one of these addresses is given below :—

Dear brother Mr. Vir Chandra Raghav Gandhi.

We, the members of the Shri Hem Chandracharya Abhyas Society, have met together to express our feelings of joy and sorrow-joy at the thought that you are going to such a distant country for the dissimination of tenets of Jainism, and sorrow because we will be deprived of the assistance of such a useful member.

Dear brother, at a time when there was very little education among our community, you passed the highest collegiate examinations and displayed too deep an interest in spiritual and worldy matter to be adequately spoken of. The strenuous efforts you made in connection with the holy places of pilgrimage such as Shri Satrunjaya and Samedshikhar etc., are highly commendable.

In 1893 you went as a representative of Shri Muniraj Atmaramji on behalf of the Jain community to the Parliament of Religions in America.

The Muniraj is one of those selfless men who are always devoted to the interests of the Jain community and who have pledged from the day of their initiation to the end of their lives to perpetually preaching the highest truths of Jainism. He is one of the greatest preachers of the Jain religion and scholars of its literature–the preacher and scholar whose premature death is mourned by the whole community–the equal of whom in erudition and the knowledge of Jaina Shastras is difficult to find to succeed him and whose holy and virtuous deeds will for ever be remembered with undying gratitude by the present and the coming generations. The speeches which you have delivered in America on Jain religion & philosphy have done immense good to us and our American brethren. It is very gratifying that on this occasion of your going for the second time in response to the invitation of our American brethren, you are also taking your wife with you. Her resolve in going with you on this occasion justifies in its fullest sense the significance of the word "Sahcharni" a constant companion.

In conclusion, dear brother, our prayer is that happiness and prosperity may attend you while you are abroad, that success may crown the mission which you have voluntarily undertaken, that blessings may be showered upon you and that you may achieve distinction.

Gentlemen, it is my humble request that if there is any error in the book due to my shortcomings or inadvertence or misprinting, it may kindly be corrected, and that I may be informed of the same so that I may correct it in the next edition.

Jaswant Rai Jaini,
Lahore.

CHICAGO PRASHNOTTARA.

OR

Questions and answers on Jainism for the Chicago Parliament of Religions.

---

1. Salutation be to Him who is devoid of all blemishes and full of all virtues whether He be *Brahmâ*, *Vishnu*, *Shiva* or a *Jina*.

2. O Bhagavân, let you be what you are by name and condition in this or that period; if you are the same entirely devoid of sin and contamination, let my reverence be to you.

3. He whom the Shaivaities adore as Shiva, the Vedântins as Brahma, the Buddhists as Buddha, the rationalistic Naiyayikas as creator, the learned Jainâs as Arhat and the Mimansikas as Eternal Action : may such a one—the Crest—jewel (Supreme one) of the three worlds realise our hearts' desire.

Q—(1) Has Ishvara or God any beginning ?

A.—Godhead has no beginning because that which has a beginning has of necessity two causes-material and instrumental causes. Neither of these two causes can be established in regard to Godhead *ergo* Godhead is beginningless. Ishvara or God is nothing but the attainment of the stage of liberation which souls have either with or without bodies attained in the immemorial past or will obtain in the future. The state of liberation and God are identical.

2. Q.—How have people come to believe that there is God ?

A.—Almost all believers in God have come to this belief by observing various types of the wonderful creation of the world which they say cannot but be attributed to a Being of infinite power who is the creator and called God. This argument has led people to believe that there is God but it is fallacious, because both sentient and insentient beings are potential with infinite powers, which combining with each other by the operation of the five forces *i. e.*, Time, Nature, Function, uninterrupted Activity and Motive power have been evolving and dissolving this variegated universe from eternity.

This universe full of sentient and insentient beings has been in continuous manifestation and is therefore beginningless. Hence the argument proving the existence of God as creator, falls to the ground.

3. Q.—What do ancient scriptures say regarding the belief in God ?

A.—The Jain scriptures declare the Tirthankaras, who, free from eighteen short-comings, have attained liberation in their bodies and the Siddhas or the perfect who have attained that liberation after the dissolution of their bodies, to be God or Ishvara.

These stages of liberation with and without bodies are called Ishvara. The ancient Sankhya scripture does not believe in God. The modern Sankhya doctrine designated Seshvaravâdi declares Mahadeo to be God. The followers of Jaimani's doctrine donot believe in God. The followers of Uttarmimânsâ *i.e.* the Vedantic doctrine, believe in panthesim or the doctrine of regarding all that is in the world to be God. The followers of Nyaya and Vaisheshik doctrines believe in God who is One, Omnipresent, eternal, an everlasting abode of wisdom, omniscient, the dispenser of the fruits of the good and bad actions of beings and who consigns them to hell and heaven.

The followers of Budhism believe in a God who is the preacher of their four eternal truths *viz.*, existence of Sorrow or Misery, cause of suffering, cessation of sorrow and the path that leads to that cessation, and who incarnates himself in the world whenever his teaching is neglected.

4. Q.—What do reasoning and scriptures say in regard to the existence of God ?

A.—The reasoning in establishing the existence of God is simply this. There are two kinds of words or expressions simple and compound. The examples of simple words are pot, cloth, soul, virtue, merit, sin, liberation, spirit, and those of compound words are cows' horns, buffaloes' horns, Raja's son, or hare's horns, man's horns, barren woman's son. The thing denoted by a simple word necessarily exists while the thing or things denoted by a compound word or expression may or may not exist. Ishvara or God is a simple word ; hence it necessarily exists. *

As regards the view of the scriptures, the Jain Shastras hold that their Arhantas who have become Siddhas are ; Gods.

The Buddhists consider Buddha to be their God. The followers of Nyaya and Vaisheshik doctrine consider Shiva to be God and the Vedas consider the manifested creation to be the God.

* NOTE.—Just as pot etc., the word "Ishvara" is a simple word, having meaning, derivation and existence. If it is meaningless it can have no derivation, nor can it be correct just as the words Dith &c. The word "Ishvara" is not like these words; it has therefore meaning. If it has no derivation it cannot have any meaning though it is correct just as Dith &c. If a compound word has a derivation, it cannot have a pure meaning just as the words Khari-Vishana (horns of an ass).

5. Q.—What proof is there that God is the creator and the protector of the world ?

A.—There is no direct or indirect proof establishing that God is the creator and protector of this world.

6. Q.—What fallacy is there in believing that Ishvara is the creator of the world and of all things ?

A.—There are several fallacies in maintaining this view.

7. Q.—Yours indeed is a curious statement. I have never heard that there is any fallacy in maintaining that God is the creator of the world. Please point out the fallacy in the view.

A.—Friend, tell me what sort of God you believe in, as the creator of the world.

8. Q.—Are there many kinds of Ishvara (God) ?

A.—Do you not know that they believe in two kinds of God. One kind of God existed before the creation ; there was no other material cause or being then.

There was only one pure, intelligent, and blissful existence. This is what one class of people believe in. The other class believe in the beginninglessness or eternal existence of God pure, intelligent and of blissful existence, soul, atom, space, time, directions or quarters, (altogether nine substances) &c. of which the universe is made up. Both these existences are believed to be eternal. Which of these two views about God do you hold?

9. Q.—I hold the first view about God because the Vedas and the other scriptures declare thus.*

---

* NOTE.—From this spirit emanated Ether; from ether emanated air; from air, fire; from fire, water; from water, earth; from earth, herbs; from herbs, food; from food, semen; from semen, man; the man is thus made up of food and fluid. Tattriaya Sakha.

O dear, He alone was in the beginning-one without a second; He saw and the multifarious beings were born. Chandogya Upanishad.

Neither was it nor was it not; nor was it existent nor non-existent &c. &c. Rigveda.

Atma alone was in the beginning-not anything else. It saw and the beings were borne. Aitraya Brahman.

All these texts declare that there was only one God before the creation. There was then neither the world nor the creator of the world. There was only one pure existence *i. e.* God. Christians and Mohammadans also hold this view. I too maintain the same opinion.

A.—This view of yours renders the God imperfect.

10. Q.—How is God rendered imperfect if he is said to be the creator of the universe ?

A.—In the first place there is no material cause of the universe, hence it can never be created, for that which has no material cause can never come into existence just as the horns of an ass.

11. Q.—God has created the universe out of His own power or nature. The material cause of the world is therefore God's power.

A. (1)—Is the power of God separate or inseparate from him ?

If it is separate from Him, is it sentient or insentient?

If insentient, then is it eternal or non-eternal?

If eternal, then your statement that there was only one God before the creation and no other existence, is like the statement of a mad man. It is self-contradictory. If you call that power non-eternal, then its material cause must be another power of God which must also have another power for its cause and so on and so forth. This is an argument in a circle and involves a fallacy. If you call it a sentient power, then is it eternal or non-eternal? In both the cases the above two fallacies *i. e.*, self-contradiction and reasoning in a circle arise. If you consider this power non-separate from God, then all things are God. Every thing becomes God *i. e.*, good and evil; heaven and hell; merit and demerit; virtue and vice; the high and the low; the king and the beggar; the virtuous and the wicked; the ruler and the ruled; a good man and a thief; the happy and the unhappy &c. &c.

If that is the case, then instead of creating the universe He has brought on His own ruin. This is the first stigma on God.

(2.) When Ishvara has become everything, then what is the use of his creating the Vedas and other scriptures and what is the use of reading them. This is another imperfection of Him.

(3.) If these Vedas and other scriptures were created for His own knowledge, then he must be without knowledge before creation. This is the third fallacy.

(4.) He is proved to have become impure from being pure and to have undergone the labour of creating the universe which is fruitless. This is the fourth fallacy.

(5.) The fifth objection arises that no distinction between good and evil is proved.

(6.) The sixth objection is ;—Why has He involved Himself in this difficulty. In this way you impute many imperfections to God.

12. Q.—God is omnipotent ; hence he can

produce the universe without any material cause.

A.—This answer of yours cannot satisfy any wise man, because it is totally unsupported by any proof. That which has no material cause can never come into existence, for instance ass' horns. Argument like this is liable to weaken, rather than strengthen your position. If you insist upon the things of your own imagination out of prejudice you can never be considered a critic. Your statement involves a fallacy of mutual dependance. If one pure existence of God not depending upon any material cause before the creation be premised, then only can He be proved Omnipotent, and when He is proved Omnipotent He can be said to have created the universe without any material cause. Until one of these two propositions is established, the other cannot be proved. This is reasoning in a circle. The two propositions are either to prove the creator of the universe or to prove God Omnipotent. When He is proved omnipotent, then can He be proved to have created the universe without any material cause. When He is proved to be the creator of the universe, then only can He be proved omnipotent. Is not this reasoning in a circle ?

13. Q.—The existence of God is self-evident. Why do you not consider Him as the creator of the universe ?

A.—If the creation of the universe by God is proved self-evident, then none can have any dispute about it and our controversy about God may also cease because what is self evident admits of no argumentation. But that the presence of God cannot be known by direct perception, has been laid down in your Vedas.*

This Vedic verse evidently shows that God cannot be cognised by any one.

14. Q. How has the world come into existence without a creator ? This inferential proof establishes that God is the

* NOTE.—Without feet and hands, He walks and grasps, without eyes He sees, without ear, He hears; He knows the universe best but there is none in the universe who knows Him. He is called the primeval ancient Purusha.

creator of the world—Why do you not accept this ?

A.—We shall refute this argument of yours when dealing with the other aspect of God. Although it is not proved that there was only one God before the creation without any material causes, even then we proceed on and ask whether these souls when created by God were Pure, (2) whether they were endowed with merits, (3) whether they were impregnated with sins, (4) whether they were mixed with virtue and sin together, (5) whether they had more sin and less virtue and (6) whether they had more virtue and less sin.

If you maintain the first position, then all the souls in the world ought to be pure and all the injunctions of the scriptures regarding them ought to be futile. Besides, the author of these scriptures is also proved to be unwise; for it was useless to compose these scriptures for the guidance of the souls which were already pure. No sensible man washes a clean cloth ; if he does so, he is a fool. This shows that if these scriptures were put together for the guidance of pure souls, the author thereof was not a wise man.

15. Q.—God created all the souls pure, but they, out of their own will, did good or bad actions. How is God to be blamed for this ?

A.—When Ishvara did not endow the souls with a power to do good or evil actions, how have they then come into possession of that power ?

16. Q.—God has created all powers in the souls but He does not prompt them to do evil to which they are led of their own accord. Suppose a man gives his dear child a toy to play with but the child injures his eye with it, are the parents to blame for it ? Similarly God has given hands, feet, and other organs of actions to beings only for the performance of virtuous actions. If one did evil of his own accord ; is God to blame for it ?

A.—O simple-minded man, the example of a child which you have given is not correct because the parents of the child do not know that the toy they have given will be so used by him as to injure his eye. If the parents knew this they would never give the toy to the child. If they give it knowingly, they are not his parents but his enemies.

Similarly according to your theory, God is to be regarded as our parent and we are all his children. If He knew that the man who has been given hands, feet, mind, and other senses, would use them so as to commit sins leading him to hell, He would not have created him. If He did not know this, He is proved to be devoid of wisdom and omniscience. If He knew this, the charge of His being our enemy is brought against Him. What was His object in getting so many men doing things which would lead them to hell? God is proved to be unjust in as much as He has supplied man wherewithal to do sin, and then punished him for doing so.

God is thus proved to be unjust, parvi-scient, cruel and unwise. Since it would not be advisable to bring so many charges against Him, it would be better to accept that God did not create sinless souls. This is an answer to your first proposition ; and as regards your Second proposition, the refutation is as follows :—

If you say that God has created only virtuous souls, then the objection is, why are men born blind, lame, cripple, deaf, deformed, and also in low and penury-stricken families ?

Certainly the after-effects of virtue do not make men miserable and starving for life and to be drudging for mouthfuls of food. Besides, how could God make the souls virtuous without their having done good deeds before. If He made them virtuous without their previous deeds, He might as well send them to heaven or give them salvation without their doing any virtuous deeds. When it was so easy, why did God create the difficulty of men undergoing such ordeals as the following in obedience to scriptural injunctions:—keeping fasts, abandonment of greed, passion and animosity, enrolment in the order of ascetics, anchorites, mendicants &c., adherence to the virtues of compassion, self control, charity, truthfulness, abstinence from theft and the company of women. Does it not show that God is neither discrect nor wise ?

As regards the 3rd objection, the answer is as follows :—

If you say that God created the souls encrusted with sin, then does it not show that the souls were charged with sins without having done them ? When the God Himself has ruined us, to whom else are we to represent our grievances to the effect that we have been charged with sin by God without our having committed them and soliciting his aid in keeping God from doing so. The unjust God who charges us with sins without our committing them ought never to be adored. If God had created all the souls encrusted with sin, a birth in the family of kings, ministers, order to attain heaven and salvation ;— military commanders, and millionares, healthy body excellent, form and person, respect at home, and fame abroad, enjoyment of all the five senses &c. &c. would be impossible. Therefore God has not created sinful men.

A.—To the 4th proposition.—If you say that the souls were created half sinful and half virtuous, the statement is equally preposterous because all souls are not seen half happy and half miserable in the world.

A.—To the 5th proposition.—This position too is not tenable in asmuch as it is not found that the majority of beings is happy and the minority miserable, on the other hand, the majority is found to be in misery and the minority in happiness. Under these circumstances, it is established that God could not create the souls in any condition ; *ergo* He could not be the creator. Was God unhappy before the creation, and happy after it ?

17. Q.—God is always happy. He had no deficiency in order to make up which, He created this world. He creates the universe in order to manifest His glory.

A.—Was not the glory of God manifest before He created the universe ? If His glory was not manifest before the creation, God must be in a gloomy mood and anxious about the attainment of His desire and to manifest His glory.

God must therefore be in misery. If He was miserable before the creation why did He remain idle and why did He not remove His misery by creating another universe before this universe.

18. Q.—God has created the universe with the object that the souls may do virtuous deeds and attain unending happiness. He created the universe to do good to others.

A.—If it is doing good to others to make them do good deeds and attain happiness, what act of goodness is His towards those who have gone to the hell after committing sins ?

19. Q.—Can God be called philanthropic by making the latter unhappy? He would take them out of the hell and send them to heaven.

A.—Why did He allow them to go to hell first?

20. Q.—It is God who makes men do virtuous or sinful deeds. They cannot do anything of themselves. Just as a puppet dancer makes puppets dance as he likes, so does God make people do what He wills.

A—If it is not in the power of souls to do anything, they should not be responsible for good or bad results. If a master orders his servant to do anything and the servant does it in obedience to his order and the result turns out to be bad, would the master punish the servant for it? No, never. Similarly if men do good or bad actions in obedience to God's orders they cannot be held responsible for their results. When men have not done good or bad actions, they cannot go to heaven or hell nor can they attain any of the four conditions of life such as

(1) heaven (2) hell (3) human life and (4) animal, mineral and vegetable life. When there are no such four conditions of life there is no universe. When there is no universe there are no such scriptures as the Vedas, Purânas, Qurân, Tauret, Jabur, Bible &c. When there are no scriptures, there are no religious teachers. When there are no religious teachers, there is no God. When there is no God there is universal void. How can this absurdity be dealt with ?

21. Q.—This universe is like the show of a juggler aud God acts like a juggler. By the creation of this universe God simply amuses Himself by His tricks. There are no such things as heaven, hell, virtue and sin.

A.—If God has created the world simply for His amusement, the results thereof ought to be simply like the effects of a juggler's performance. But in this world there are men who are sick, leprous, grief-stricken, penniless, infirm and extremely wretched wallowing in the depths of squalor and misery. The very sight of these persons evokes our compassion and excites our horripilation. Does not the sight of these miserable creatures move God with pity ? If God is not moved with pity, He cannot be God. The performer of a trick is like a foolish child full of passion and animosity. If He is affected by passion and hatred He is full of all defects. When He is full of all defects He cannot be God. He can only be a worldly man. He who has passion and hatred cannot be omniscient and He who is not omniscient can never be called God.

22. Q.—God rewards or punishes men according to their actions therefore He is not to blame. As one soweth so does one reap.

A.—Your statement proves that the world is beginningless and God is not its creator. Bravo ! you have undermined your own position yourself. You are coming to the position that whatever condition the living beings have in this life, are the results of their deeds in the previous life and what they were in the previous life, was the result of their actions in the one preceding it. In this way the chain goes back ad-infinitnm. This argument proves that the world is beginningless and that God is not its creator.

23. Q.—I believe only in one supreme Brahma who is an ever existing reality

A.—If there is only one Supreme Brahma of ever-existing reality then does it not follow from this that all these variegated phenomena such as pine tree, mango tree, sugar cane, palm tree &c &c are unreal?

24. Q.—All this phenomenon is unreal. All that appears is unreal. Nothing more real than the appearance of silver in a mother of pearls (fish, shell). There is only one Supreme Brahma who is perpetually real.

A.—Your statement does not point to your keen intelligence. There are three kinds of unrealities. One that is substantially untrue, the other which appears different from what it really is and the third which is indescribable unreality. Which of these unrealities do you believe in?

25. Q.—I do not believe in the first two kinds of unrealities. I believe in the third kind of unreality which is indescribable. The phenomena are indescribably unreal.

A.—Please let me know first what you mean by the word indescribable. (1) Does it mean that the word does not denote any object? (2) Does it mean that the object which the word denotes has no existence?

The first position is not worth considering seriously because it is evidently proved that such things as trees &c do exist. As regards the 2nd position it has to be ascertained whether the knowledge of the object or the object itself which the word denotes does not exist. The first case is wrong because the knowledge of such objects as pine tree, mango tree, palm tree &c &c, is possessed by men. As regards the existence or non-existence of the object itself it has again to be ascertained whether the positive or negative existence is meant. If you say that there is no positive existence of things and yet they appear, you will be driven on to the fallacy of Perverse Knowledge and this fallacy is held highly objectionable by those who believe in advaitism. If you say that objects are devoid of non-existence, then you come to their having a positive existence which involves the canon of Real Existence of phenomena.

If you believe in Advaitism and also accept the statement involved in the above dogma of real existence you are directly against Advaitism which in that case can never be established.

26. Q.—Objects have neither existence nor non-existence.

A.—Do you accept the usual meanings of the terms existence and non-existence or attach some other meaning of your own to them. If you accept the usual sense of these terms you will have to admit that where a thing does not exist it is non-existent and when it exists it is not non-existent- These two propositions are contradictory. If you reject one you must admit the other. Here is no scope for are indescribable unreality. If you attac your own meaning to these terms, the matter does not affect us because when the term and the object denoted by it appear in the artificial sense you have imposed on them the usual sense of the word and the object denoted by it would never be absent. How would you then prove the phenomena to be indescribably unreal? If the indescribable unreality is not proved, how can phenomena be proved unreal. Nor can only one Brahma be proved.

27. Q.—I call that to be indescribable which is not visible.

A.—Your position is highly self-contradictory. If the phenomena are not visible, why did you accept them as visible and having attributes in your former statement. If you ask what contradiction there is in accepting them as visible and having attributes, then your statement that what is not visible is indescribable would fall through. When the phenomena are not indescribable, then either they would be existing in form or non-existing in form. In accepting either of these two positions you will again be driven on to either of the two fallacies of "Perverse Knowledge" and "Real Existence" alluded to above. I ask you again whether your belief in holding the phenomena as indescribable is based on direct or indirect proof. The direct proof shows the phenomena as they appear *i. e.*, really existing. As are the objects, so is their cognition by direct proof and each object of the phenomena is existing in regard to its own form and non-existent in regard to other objects. All these objects existing separately from one another form what is called Prapanchor Phenomena. This being the case how it is possible on the basis of direct evidence to prove the phenomena to be indescribable.

28. Q.—The direct evidence cannot rebut my former position on the other hand it strengthens it. If direct evidence were to show that the nature of one object does not exist in another object then it would weaken my position.

The direct evidence is not of this nature

as it does not show that the nature of one object does not exist in another object.

A.—Your statement is untenable. You cannot have the knowledge of the true nature of an object without nagativing the nature of a different object in it. You can have an idea of blue colour only when you nagative in it yellow or other colours. When you become cognisant of the real nature of an object by direct proof, then only you can deny the existence of other objects therein. You cannot know the true nature of an object unless you realise the negation of another object therein. In fact to realize the true nature of an object is to negative the existence of a different object in it. When the direct proof admits of both existence and non-existence of an object, the phenomena can never be proved real. When the phenomena cannot be proved real, the Supreme spirit who is only one without the second cannot be proved. If you considered the direct evidence proving only the existence of things you will also have to admit the existence of nescience just like the existence of knowledge. Your statement that Brahm is proved without nescience by direct evidence also shows the negation of nescience by the same proof. It being so, your statement that direct proof indicates only existence and not non-existence is like the statement of a madman. Now as regards your indirect proof what is argued later on will repudiate it. My position is that the phenomena are not an illusion being opposed to unreality. What is opposed to unreality is real such as the soul. Similar is the case with the phenomena. Your argument relating to the cognition of things is opposed to the existence of Supreme being in asmuch as the Supreme spirit is not perceptible but at the same time not unreal. If you say that the supreme spirit is imperceptible then it is indescribable. If it is not indescribable, your position becomes untenable, because your expostulation is that there is nothing else besides the Brahma and that the supreme *Atman* is invisible. In your former argument you gave an example of a mother of pearl. That example is inapplicable in asmuch as the mother of pearl is included in the phenomena which you consider to be unreal. An example ought to refer to a thing which is capable of being proved. It is not yet proved whether the existence of the mother of pearl is real or unreal. Such being the case you cannot give an example of it. Further I ask you whether the argument you put forward to prove the unreality of phenomena is included in the phenomena or not? If not included, is it real or unreal ? If real, then the phenomena too like your argument, are also real. If unreal, is it a void or an example of "Perverse knowledge" or something inexpressible ? The first two propositions are not conducive to what is to be proved ; they are just as the horns of a man or the silver in a mother of pearl. As regards the third statement relating to indescribability, it cannot in the first place be possibly thought of, then it cannot prove the point at issue.

29. Q.—My proposition is true from a common sense view ; therefore it cannot be wrong and is calculated to prove its object.

A.—I ask you to let me know the form of this common sense view. The word Vyavahara derived from its root means nothing else than knowledge. Whatever is real by means of knowledge is intrinsically real. This view proves the phenomena to be real. When the phenomena are real, it cannot be said that only one supreme Brahma without a second is real and all else unreal. If you say that the use of the word is true, I ask you whether the word is real or unreal. If you say that the word is real, then the phenomena are as well real as the word. If you say that the word is unreal, such words as Brahm &c cannot be real because that which is itself unreal cannot be the cause of anything that is real.

30. Q.—Just as a false coin points to the transactions in genuine coins, so does our view though false, point to the reality of

the phenomena. It therefore proves its object.

A.—O ! friend your statement makes your argument really false. All the fallacies pointed out in connection with the unreality of the phenomena, would again arise here. If you argue that you do not consider your reasoning separate from the phenomena, your reasoning is certainly unreal like the phenomena and it cannot prove its point. What has been explained before does not prove the phenomena to be unreal, they are real like souls and your position that only one Brahma without a second is real and all else false, falls to the ground.

31. Q.—It is declared in the Upanishads as well as stated by Anandagiri, the disciple of Shankara Swami in the third chapter of the "Shankara - dig-vijaya" that the Supreme spirit is the material cause of the universe. The material cause is that which transforms itself into effect. This shows that whatever there is in the

universe is the transformation of the Supreme spirit. The universe thus being the form of the Supreme spirit, what objection is there that God is the creator of the universe?

A.—You are certainly the prince of atheists. Do you at all consider what you say? Your statement shows your position to be atheistic. When the world is the transformation of the Supreme Being, then there are no such things as a sinner, a virtuous man, a sage, a fool, the heaven or the hell, a good man, or a thief, truthful or untruthful scriptures &c. &c. From this point of view there is no difference between a beef eater and a corn eater, no difference between an act of sexual intercourse with one's wife and that with one's other relatives, no difference between an ascetic and an ass, because when God is the material cause of all things, the whole world is of one essence and form as there nothing else.

32. Q.—I believe in Brahma and Mâyâ. Whatever arguments and theories you have propounded are the products of Mâyâ. Brahma is one ever lasting, conscious, blissful and pure existence.

A.—O! Believer in monism! the position which you have now taken up is extremely wrong. Is Mâyâ separate or non-separate from the Brahma? If separate, is it sentient or insentient? If insentient, is it eternal or transitory. If you say that it is eternal it uproots the monistic creed because when it is separate from God and is insentient and ever lasting it means that you have yourself admitted the truth of the dualistic theory and undermined that of the monistic doctrine. If you say that Mâyâ is transitory even then you cannot do away with dualism, because whatever is perishable is an effect and an effect is another form of cause, and on this statement the material cause of Mâyâ cannot be shown. If you say that the cause of the Mâyâ is another Mâyâ, you reason in a circle and the monistic theory remains unproved If you consider Brahma to be the material cause of the universe, it means that everything is Brahma which involves the fallacy already alluded to above. If you consider Mâyâ to be sentient, the same fallacy applies to it as well. If you consider Mâyâ to be inseparate from God, then it is sufficent to speak only of Brahma and not of another superfluous entity.

33.—Q. I consider Mâyâ to be indescribable.

A.—The argument about the indescribability of existence has already been repudiated. The prefix *Nis* in the term "Anirvachniya" (indescribable) means negation and the remaining portion of it according to the Kalapik Vyâkarana (Grammar) means either existence or non-existence. If you deny existence, non-existence is proved and if you deny non-existence, existence is proved. There is nothing else than existence and non-existence. The term "Anirvachniya" or "Indescribable" seems to have been invented only as a trade trick. By that word, only the dualistic theory is proved, not the monistic one.

34. Q.—The Vedic texts such as "God alone is the creator of all" prove only the monistic theory.

A.—This statement of yours is also untrue. If the whole mankind is of one essence and form, then all phenomena such as one being happy and another miserable &c.&c., will become eventually unreal. If this is your position, then the statement that "the world having been found to be useless, one should avoid and evade it" would be as meaningless as speaking of the fragrance of sky flowers. If there is only one essence without a second, there is no such thing as rebirth of souls in this world which is to be avoided as some thing useless and abominable.

35. Q.—In reality there is nothing else than Brahma and the universe which has now been declared useless and which is always visible to all the beings is just like the appearance of the limbs &c., of a woman

in a picture. It is to be seen whether the dimensions of the limbs of the woman in the picture are illusionary or productive of illusion.

A.—What you say is all wrong. There is in fact no proof supporting your statement. If in order to prove only one Brahma without anything else, you resort to some other distinct evidence you only prove Dualism, because, without any proof no one's position is proved. If you consider a thing proved without any proof, then all religionists can prove their self-believed creeds. A mirage or illusion should be considered separate from the Advaitism, which you consider to have been proved.

The theory of Advaitism which you have established will thus be disproved. If illusion is only a form of Advaitism it is necessarily a form of the Brahma. If the mirage or illusion is a form of the Brahma, the knowledge about elements can never be proved. If you consider illusion to be separate from Brahma you come to believe in Dualism and the monistic theory is damaged. If you consider the belief in the distinction between a pillar and a pot to be illusion, then it means that the pot &c. has a real existence somewhere, so long as the reality is not seen one cannot form the idea of illusion or unreality. He who has not seen a live serpent can never have the illusion of a serpent in a rope.

This too repudiates the monistic reality. The monistic theory is certainly to be preached to others and not to one's ownself as the preacher is himself without any illusion or perverted knowledge. If the preacher is himself affected with illusion he cannot prove the monistic theory to others.

36. Q Since the soul is affected with illusion or perverted knowledge it is necessary to preach the monistic theory.

A.—When the illusion of the soul is gone,

it will certainly change its condition and when there is such a change, Dualism comes in of itself. When a man preaches Advaitism to another man it is taken for granted that another man exists. To be preaching monism to another man and at the same time believing in its truths is just like saying that one's father has been a celibate from his birth. Certainly such a man is devoid of all sense. Believing in the existence of oneself and of another is nothing else than Dualism. To believe in monism is therefore destitute of all reasoning.

37. Q—The existence of one Supreme soul is enough to show the baselessness of all knowledge relating to differences.

NOTE:—If the serpent has not been seen before, how can it be seen in a rope. It is owing to the previous observation or non-observation that illusion or non-illusion occurs.

A.—This argument of yours is also wrong in asmuch as the existence of one Supreme soul has not been proved.

If there is such an existence is it self-evident or proved by the help of some other evidence? It is not self-evident for if it were so, none could have any controversy about it. If it is proved by means of other evidence, is that evidence empirical or scriptural? If this evidence is empirical, what is the argument? Please explain.

38. Q—The argument is this that the matter which is under discussion relates to the interpenetration of the Brahma in the outward phenomena, because whatever appearances there are, have for their background some underlying principle.

In other words all phenomena have nomena behind them, just as the functions of the body which are outwardly apparent have the soul for their underlying principle. Since all sentient and insentient phenomena are under consideration their outward appearance cannot be accounted for without there being some underlying principle behind them. The instances of a pot, a piece of cloth, &c. &c. are illustrative of this position.

A.—This argument of yours is not correct because the existence of the subject matter to be proved, the reasoning proving it and the example illustrating it, is only by way of proof.

39. Q—There are two kinds of (1) one God—the material cause of the universe and (2) matter which is eternal. The matter consists of the atoms of Earth, Water, Fire, and Air, and of Space, Direction, Soul, mind and time. These nine substances are eteanal and beginningless—not made by any one. With the aid of these God creates the world.

The manner in which God is considered the Creator of the world by religionists is this. "He is one-the creator of the world. He is omnipresent, eternal and self-dependent. He is the Lord of this visible world and its multitudes of beings."

Those who believe in the creation of the world by God hold that the earth, mountains, trees &c. in asmuch as they are effects, are the work of an intelligent

Being. The world is a product just like a pot. It is therefore the production of an intelligent Being who is none else than God. If you say that this argument is untenable because the earth, mountains, trees &c. are produced by the combination of their innate causes and are therefore effects, and have bodies ; this is not right. Nor can it be said that this argument is manysided and contradictory as it is very remote from the position of the opponents. Nor can it be urged that this argument is beyond the basis of Time as the direct evidence is not barred by the scripture-the subject and its attributes being different. Nor can it be said that this argument is not cognate as what is to be proved is not established by the absence of the contrary proposition. Nor can it be said that God is not the creator of the world because of His having no body and being just as a liberated soul. There is a conflict between the first and second propositions which does not allow the statement that God is the creator of the world, to be established. By denying a body to God, He has not been proved the creator of the world. We believe in God having a body and therefore our proposition is correct. God is only one. If there were many Gods, there would be a divergence of views among them in the accomplishment of a work (taken up by all simultaneously). As there is none else to check them their differences will continue and the accomplishment of the work be interfered with.

The case would be that one God is creating a man with four legs, another with six legs, the third, with two legs and the fourth, with eight legs. In this manner all other things will be made variously. There would in such a case be general confusion and disorder in the world.

But no such disorder is seen ; hence the creator is only one God. God is also omnipresent and omniscient. If God were not omnipresent, the things which would be created simultaneously in all the three worlds, would never be created at the same time because only where potters are present, pots will be made and not where they are not present. God. is omniscient. If He were not so, He could not be able to know the material causes of all the products. If He did not know the material causes of the products He would not create a variety among the objects. God is self-dependent not relying upon any one else. He dispenses fruits of happiness or sorrow by His own will. "It is by the will of God that the worldly beings go to heaven or hell. Without Him they are unable to reward or punish themselves for their virtuous or wicked deeds."

If God is dependent upon some one else, then He will not be regarded as the chief author of the world. There will also come in the fallacy of argument in a circle if one God is dependent upon another and another upon the third and so on and so forth.

God is therefore self-dependent—not under the control of some one else. God is eternal. If He were non-eternal, some one else is required to create Him. There is no other such Being; therefore God is eternal. It will thus be observed that God is the creator of the world.

A.—Your statement that the earth, mountains, trees, &c. are the work of an intelligent Being, is untenable, for your proposition does not recognise the quality of "pervasion." The inference is not valid till supported by the evidence of "perva sion." What I say is recognised by all learned men. Now I ask you whether the God that creates has a body or no. If He has a body, is His body visible just like ours or invisible like the body of ghosts &c? If you consider that He has a body like ours, then it involves the fallacy of the infringement of direct evidence, as Grass, trees, rainbow, clouds &c. are seen being produced without the presence of God. If you accept the other statement, then the body ofGod is invisi ble. I ask whether this body is invisible by the reason of its grandeour or by reason of our vitiated sight which is the result of our previous bad actions. For the statement that the body of God is invisible owing to its transcendent glory, there is no proof. Besides your statement has the fallacy of mutual dependence. When it is proved that His glory is transcendent, then only is proved the invisibility of His body and vice versa.

If the body of God is that of a ghost, then the matter will remain as doubtful as it was. The question will be whether there is any God at all as His body is invisible. Either it is not in existence just as the son of a barren woman or it is the gloom of our past action which obstructs our vision. Such doubts will never cease. If you say that God is without a body, then the illustration and the one whose illustration is given will be mutually inconsistent and the argument will be self-destructive, because the author of effects such as pots &c. is a potter with a visible body. If you call God without a body, He will be found incompetent to do anything. Just as the vacuum of the sky is without any maker, so God either with or without body cannot be proved as associated with the effects of the world. Besides your argument is not all comprehensive in asmuch as you admit that there is no intelligent author of such effects as lightning, clouds, rainbow &c. Your argument vitiated as it is, does not prove that an intelligent God is the creator of the world. The statement that the whole world is the work of God is not tenable, for, there is no evidence to prove that God is the creator of the world.

Q.—Evidence proving God to be the creator of the world is of the character of nuinference. One who dispenses fruits to beings according to their actions must be an intelligent judge. Tools such as an axe or a saw gradually cut a piece of wood into two under the supervision of an artizan, so do the good or evil consequences of actions take effect under the direction of an intelligent judge. It can never be said that such tools as an axe and a saw move themselves to cut up a piece of wood because they are insentient objects. If it is said that it is the nature of the axe and the saw to cut, then they should always be cutting and never cease. This is not the case. By this example it is proved that the different souls attain their fruits gradually under the direction of God-just as circular triangular and rectangular villages and towns are the work of an intelligent town-planner. As are pots &c. exactly so are the earth, mountains, trees &c. the work of God.

A.—The inferential proof by which you establish that God is the creator of the world is not sound as it suffers from the fallacy of taking for granted what is to be proved. It is just like what has already been refuted by me. The view held by the Jains as heretofore alluded to, is that the variety that we see in the world is due to the effects of actions. Karma or action alone is the cause of the conditions of happiness or sorrow of the various kinds of people inhabiting India, and all other countries, islands, and cold mountainous tracts. There is nothing else than Karma. Form experience too, Karma is found to be the prime cause. When a virtuous king reigns, there is neither famine nor any other distress and this happy state is justly considered as due to the influence of his righteous actions. That which gradually gives reward or punishment to beings is Karma and Karma only. Actions depend up on men who being sentient beings are intelligent. It is therefore that actions being dependent upon rational beings gradually unfold their effects. If you say that your aim is to prove only a super-intelligent God, and not ordinary intelligent beings, then your proposition is devoid of what is to be proved. The connection of God as a supervisor in regard to the action of an axe, or a saw is not established but the connection of potters and others in regard to making pots &c. is established.

41. Q. Even great men are led to their work

by the promptings of God. My proof does not suffer from the fallacy of taking for granted what is to be proved.

A.—If it is so, then God will require another God to prompt Him to action, and that God, a third God to move him on and so on and so forth. Such a proposition involves the fallacy of reasoning in a circle.

42. Q.—Artisans &c. are ignorant ; therefore they require the prompting of God, but God being omniscient, does not require such a stimulus. My reasoning has, therefore, no fallacy.

A.—This statement is also wrong as it is mutually contradictory. You have first to prove that God has a clear knowledge of all things, then you can prove that God acts without any prompting from any other Being. When it is proved that God acts of Himself without a stimulus from some one else, then only it can be proved that God has a clear knowledge of all things. Until one of these propositions is proved, the other cannot be established. O believer in God ! I ask you how it is that God being himself omniscient and passionless, inclines men towards evil pursuits. Those who are wise, are impartial. Men ought, therefore, to be led towards good actions, not evil actions, but it is seen that God leads men even towardse vil actions. This does not prove that He is omniscient and passionless.

43. Q.—Ishwara leads all men to do good actions; therefore He is omniscient and beyond all passions. Those who do evil actions are punished by Him in this way that He inclines them to do undesireable things which lead them to hell. This is because such men may be in fear of similar troubles and be deterred from committing sin again, as He dispenses suitable fruits to men. He is wise, passionless and without any blemish.

A.—This statement is also thoughtlessly made because it is God and none else who originally inclines people to do evil. The soul itself cannot do anything because it is unintelligent and cannot do good or evil of its own accord.

To first drive people to do evil and then to throw them into the hell, thus punishing them and then taking them back to right paths, appears to be the only power of God.

44. Q.—God never drives people to do evil ; it is they themselves, who lean towards them. God dispenses fruits to men according as theyper form actions. Take, for instance, the example of a king who penalises theft and never directs a thief to commit theft. If a thief commits theft, he must be punished by the king. Similarly God does not prompt people to do evil but certainly punishes those who do evil.

A.—This argument too, is fallacious, because worldly kings however powerful, are never able to stop commission of theft altogether. Let such kings strive with all their heart, word and action to prohibit the commission of theft and similar evil deeds, but they will never succeed in keeping all men away from committing such acts. On the other hand, God is, according to you, omnipotent ; if so, why does He not keep all men away from doing evil. When God is unable to keep men away from doing evil, it is clear that God inclines them to do evil and then punshies them afterwards. This position is open to the same criticism of God as heretofore pointed out. If you say that God is unable to keep men away from doing evil, then you cannot boast loudly that God does everything and that He is omnipotent. If men perform good or bad actions themselves, then they can enjoy their fruits themselves, and it is needless to believe that God is the creator.

45. Q.—It is the men themselves who do right and wrong actions, but it is God who rewards or punishes them for them.

Men are not in a position to enjoy the fruits of their actions themselves just as thieves who commit thefts themselves are not able to punish themselves for their nefarious deeds. It is another man who sends them to a prison.

A.—This statement is also fallacious. When men are competent to do right or wrong actions, why are they not competent to enjoy their fruits themselves? According as a man does right or wrong, he becomes the cause of enjoying its fruits himself. A theif commits theft. The king punishes him or the thief is affected by such unclean diseases as leprosy, ulceration &c. It is not unoften that such a man dies being burnt by fire, or being drowned in water or being cut up by a sword or killed by a cannon ball or bullet or being destroyed by the fall of a building or a rock or is turned a starving wretch.

In various such ways, he undergoes the punishment for his evil deeds. In such a case, there is no need of the intervention of God. It is only the cause that fructifies in these evil effects and the cause is the man himself who performs the deed. Similarly there are various ways in which man undergoes punishment in hell or attains reward in heaven. If you ask what cause will lead to punishment in a case of fornication, I cannot answer, for my knowledge is limited, and cannot definitely tell the causes that will work in drawing the necessary punishment, but I can say so much that there are certainly causes which bring reward or punishment for good or evil actions. What fruit will a man attain and how and when and where, only the blessed Arhat can say. Without a cause, none can attain the consequences of his acts. It is, therefore, superfluous to bring in God for dispensation of these fruits. Can a sensible man say that a man is fit enough to cook his food but unfit to eat it. You bring in another indictment against God by considering him as the dispenser of fruits. Suppose a man is slain by a sword by another man. How was it that the slain man got his suffering and pain. Who was it that led to this suffering. If you say that it was God who drove the slayer to slay the man, then why is the slayer liable to be hanged?

Is this the law of God? He (God) first prompted the slayer to slay a man and then punished him with gallows. Your statement renders God extremely unjust. If you say that the slayer slew the man himself without any prompting from God, then it is proved that man attains reward or punishment by reason of his own acts and that no intervention of God is required as only the puny-witted men imagine. O believer in God, I ask you another question. If it is God who, for good deeds, gives one the reward of enjoyment of sexual pleasures in the company of youth-inebriated celestial nymphs, does He not at the same time punish others for misdeeds by throwing them into the fire of hell and subjecting them to various excruciating mortifications?

46. Q.—God punishes a man for the misdeeds he

has committed, for no misdeed should remain unpunished.

A.—Your statement shows that God inflicts suffering upon men unnecesarily. According to you, man cannot enjoy the fruits of their actions without the intervention of God. If He were not to punish men, they would never suffer in consequences of their deeds and thus will never be reborn or commit any further sins. What is it that leads God to roll these men again into the hell, when they are not performing any sinful actions ? An impartial and compassionate Being, never inflicts unnecessary suffering upon any man.

47. Q.—It is for his own entertainment or amusement that God sends one to heaven, and another to hell, makes one a crawling snail and another a man. When these beings skip and jump for merriment or weep or beat their breasts for sorrow, God derives enjoyment from the spectacle of his own creation. It is for this purpose that the world is created.

A.—If this is the case, God is not certainly wise. What is a mere amusement to him, involves infinite suffering to the created beings. It is unwise to call God merciful. One who is compassionate and all-knowing, never enjoys the fun consequent upon the sufferings of others. God has been said to be without passions, but now you say that he creates the world for his own enjoyment and amusement. Is amusement consistent with dispassion ? If God is dispassionate, it is impossible that he feels pleasure in such a show.

18. Q.—Our God is possessed of passion and hatred ; hence He can take pleasure in an amusement.

A.—If God has passion and hatred, He is passionate like other beings ; He is not beyond passions as alleged, neither is He omniscient. He is just like ourselves. How can He be the creator of the universe.

19. Q.—We believe in Him to be the creator of the universe, though possessed of passion and hatred.

A.—There is no proof supporting your statement that God is omniscient, notwithstanding His being possessed of passion and hatred.

50. Q.—There is no incompatability in being omniscient and being possessed of passion and hatred. Fire burns but the ether does not. The tendency to burn, that exists in fire, is not found in the ether. Similarly God is, by His disposition, both passionate and omniscient.

A.—What you say is not held by the follower of any creed. None would say that an ass which stands before him, is the creator of the world. If one asks why the ass is the creator of the world, your answer would be that it is so by its very nature. After creating the world, though omniscient and passionate, he turns into an ass. Similarly people will consider a buffalo &c. as the creator of the world. God is, therefore, only what one sets up in his imagination. This is verily a blasphemy. If God is omniscient and beyond passions, why should He create the world for His amusement ?

O Believer in God, if, according to you, everything has been created by God, then the scriptures of all faiths have been created by Him and these scriptures are contradictory to one another. Most of them are true and others untrue. God would, therefore, be considered as the preacher of both right and wrong. He is, therefore, Himself setting one against the other in religion Thousands-nay hundreds of thousands people destroy themselves by these religious dissensions. Does it not seem that God by creating the scriptures, has brought on a catastrophe on the world? The author of such false scriptures should be designated an imposter, not God. If you say that God has created only the true scriptures, not false ones which have been put together by men themselves, then it does not appear that God has created the world. It is the creatures who have created the world, and not God, because it has not been proved that God is the creator of all things in the world.

51. Q.—As to your statement that all objects having bodies are the work of an intelligent Being, I give an example and it is that an old ruined well reminds of a mason, though not present there, as in the case of a newly built well.

A.—Your positionis not correct, a cloud, a serpent's hole etc. are objects having bodies but their maker is not any intelligent Being. If you say that a cloud, the rainbow, a serpent's hole &c. are not considered to be the work of an all-intelligent. Being, then similarly the earth and mountains do not require an intelligent Being to produce them.

God is never proved to be the creator of the world on the strength of the arguments hitherto advanced. I ask those who believe God to be the creator of the world to thoroughly answer all my arguments and until they do so, they should cease believing in the God being the creator of the world. If any believers in God answer all these arguments satisfactorily, I shall feel inclined to that belief, otherwise my position holds good.

52. Q.—God is not proved to be the creator of the world. I now ask you whether it is not true that there is only one God.

A.—There is no evidence to show that there is only one God. Until such evidence is produced, the oneness of God cannot be established.

53. Q.—The argument showing the singularity of God is this. When a number of men undertake a work, it does not succeed owing to the difference of views of these men. If there were many Gods, there would be a great difference of opinions among them regarding the work of creation, which would produce confusion. Does it not therefore show that God is only One?

A.—Your reasoning does not establish the oneness of God, because God has not been proved to be the creator of any thing. Is it not strange that while a multitude of bees become of one mind in the construction of their honeycomb, Gods, who are lofty souls, immutable, immaterial, and of the forms of light, do not agree with each other. Do you consider Gods to be inferior even to insects in intelligence, knowledge and goodness as they cannot agree ?

54. Q.—The construction of the honeycomb, which a swarm of bees seem to build, is really due to the inner working of God.

A.—If it is so, then all such acts as making a pot, committing theft or fornication &c. will appear to have really been prompted by God, and man will be stripped of their responsibility.

Who will in such circumstances suffer the consequences of their deeds ? Nor will there remain any necessity of send ing men to heaven or hell.

55. Q.—It is evident that a potter, a thief or for the matter of that any other man has perfect liberty of action.

A.—Are bees alone to be debarred from having liberty of action ?. When such a difficulty comes in the way in the belief of only one God, one fails to understand how enormously would these difficulties be multiplied if there are many Gods engaged in creating the world with conflicting views, as there would be no foreman among them. One God, on seeing another God, will be jealous of his equal power and many other similar difficulties will spring up. Your argument based on the above assumption regarding the oneness of God, is really rotten and unsound. When you call God to be omniscient, it does not behove you to say that such beings will have a divergence of opinion and that they will not be of one mind.

When a God is assumed to be devoid of passions, jealousy, pride &c, how will he be affected by jealousy and pride on meeting another equally powerful God ? If such Gods were to quarrel among themselves led by jealousy and pride, they would cease to be Gods. When it is impossible to prove God to be the creator of the world, how is it possible to prove mutual bickerings among Gods in the matter? It is, therefore, free from any logical flaw to believe in a number of Gods. The assumption that God is omnipresent, is also untenable. If God is omnipresent, is he so by means of his material form or the form of knowledge?

If God pervades all by his material form, then the whole universe will be overwhelmed with the immensity of his body; no room will be left for other substances to stand. It is, therefore, impossible to think that God pervades the universe by his material form.

56. Q.—Has God any material body as shown by your argument?

A.—There are no religionists in the world, who believe that God has a material body.

57. Q.—What religions do believe in a personal God?

A.—We, the Jains, believe that one who has

attained salvation while living with his material body is a God. It is written in the Tauret that God ate bread at the house of Abraham and that he had a wrestling with Jacob. It shows that God has a body. Anandgiri—the disciple of Shankar writes in the beginning of the second chapter of Shankar-digvijaya that He is all-knowing. Anand-giri writes that when Nârad found that there had sprung up a variety of imaginary creeds and that the ancient religion had disappeared he went to Brahma and addressed him thus:—"Sire, Thy ancient religion has disappeared and in its place many a fanciful creed has sprung up. Something must be done to remove this state of affairs." On hearing this Brahma pondered over the matter a good deal and then accompanied by his sons, friends and devotees left his country and arrived at the abode of Shiva. As they approached they beheld Shiva as a radiance of millions of suns concentrated in one place but perceptible as the coolness of millions of moons. They saw he had five faces, the moon was his crown appearing as lightning above the tuft of hair. Parvati was sitting on his left side. Such was Mahadeo the Lord of all. Brahma made an obeisance to him and said, O Mahadeo, thou art omniscient, the Lord of all the world, the witness of all, the pervader of all, the first cause of all. This quotation shows that God has a body. If God had no body, how could there be five faces. This does not show that God is without body. If God has a body and is omnipresent, then his body alone will cover the whole world and another world will be required to contain all other objects. If you say that God pervades the universe by his spirit, that has yet to be proved. We too believe our Bhagvân to be omnipresent by reason of his knowledge. But your position should not be incompatible with the writings of your Vedas. In the Vedas, God is said to be omnipresent by his body. "His eyes all over the universe, His faces everywhere, His arms are outstreched all over the world, He is the beginning of the whole world." This quotation from the Vedas shows that

God pervades the universe in his material body. It being so, the fallacy previously pointed out, applies to this statement. God is not therefore omnipresent. Nor is your statement that God is omniscient, established. Why has he created us who do not believe that He is the creator of the world and act in opposition to Him? If you say that we obtain fruits according to the deeds performed by us in previous lives, then the need of God as a mediator is altogether gone. When God cannot give us anything without our previously performed actions, then God has no independance. We shall reap as we sow. If you say that God does what he likes then no one knows what He will do. Perhaps he might send the virtuous to hell and the wicked to heaven. If you say that God is just and dispenses fruits to men according to their deeds then the same fallacy as heretofore pointed out comes in. The statement that God is everlasting is equally untenable for one that is everlasting, remains unchanged in all times. If He is everlasting then it may be asked whether nature creates the world or no.

If you say that it is the nature of God to create the world, then it will prove that God will keep on perpetually creating the world *i. e.* He will never cease creating as He is endowed with the nature that always creates. If you say that it is not His nature to create the world, then God will never be in a position to create it. If God has an eternal nature to create, then there would be no Pralaya or dissolution of the universe because it is not God's nature to destroy. If you say that God's nature is twofold creative as well as destructive, then no world will ever be created or destroyed for two such powers in opposition to each other will never abide simultaneously. If they do, the world would neither be created nor destroyed, for when the creative power is creating the destructive power will be working havoc or vice versa.

This only leads one to consider that what we believe is true *i. e.* the world has neither been created by any one nor will it ever be destroyed that is eternal, as we hold. If you ask what fallacy there is in the statement that God creates and destroys the world when he is moved by creative or destructive desires then the powers of the God will be considered as non-eternal. If it is so, God is also non-eternal because God is not separated from his powers. If you maintain that His powers are separate from Him, then too the world will never be created or destroyed by reason of these powers being eternal and God will be proved as having done nothing, for, when God is separate from His powers, He is consequently unable to do anything. How will He be able to create the world? and who will be the material cause of the powers? This will only prove the non-existence of God, for, what is God stripped of His powers. He will be as imaginary as a flower in the clouds. Who will in such a case be the creator of the world?

58. Q.—If an omniscient and passionless God

is not the creator of the world, how has this world sprung up of itself. It is evident nothing is made without a maker just as a clock &c.

A.—O, enquirer. You do not seem to fully understand my argument and it is therefore you call God the creator of the world. We also hold that the finished articles that we see were made by some one, for example pot, cloth, clock, house, stall, chain &c., but such things as Sky, Time, Atoms, Soul &c. have not been made by any one. All learned man agree in the view that all things which have the forms of effects, must have material causes. Without a material cause no such effect can be produced. Only a fool can say against this view. But soul, time, atoms, and sky have no material causes and are therefore beginningless and none has made them. The statement that all things have been made by God is therefore untenable.

As regards the earth, water, fire, air plants, moving creatures, and such portions of the earth as heaven, hell, and sun, moon, planets, stars, constellations &c., these are made by the combination of matter and spirit. The earth &c. are eternal by reason of their continuity and non-eternal by their apparent forms.

The matter and spirit embodying them are of infinite potentialities. These eternal forces manifest themselves when combined with their respective causes such as time &c. and all the creation in the world that has been, is and will be, is due to the following five material causes—time, nature, continuity, action and energy. Except these five causes, no other creator or director of the world as God is proved. The line of argument refuting such an assumption has already been explained. A single seed is charged with infinite potentialities. A variety of colours, leaves, roots, fruits, bark, branches, flowers, seeds &c. &c. abide in the seed in potential forms. When the seed is burned to ashes, its potential forces reside in its atoms but none of these forces comes into manifestation without its cause or concomitant. If no such characteristic forces reside in the seed, why is it that a seed of wheat does not produce mangoes, thorns, men, animals, birds &c. All things have therefore their peculiar infinite forces. As they combine with their peculiar causes, they come into manifestation. A seed contains in miniature all the features of a tree but until it combines with its external concomitants, it does not blossom. These external concomitants are (1) rain (2) earth and water. Even if rain, earth &c. combine they cannot produce a blossom unless the seed is endowed with the potentiality to blossom. Apiece of stone, if sown will not give a blossom though all the three external causes combine. Even granting that all the four causes above mentioned exist, no blossom will come forth regularly unless the feature of continuity is combined with the forces of the seed. The previous action has also a great deal to do, for if there were no previous action to reckon with, the present form in which things are produced would not be determined. If there were no man to sow a seed or the seed itself by its gravity were not to fall on the ground, it would never put forth a blossom. Therefore there are five causes in the growth of a seed and these are (1) Time, such as rainy season (2) Nature (3) Continuity (4) Previous action and (5) Effort.

Except these five causes, no other cause, such as God, is proved in regard to the growth of a seed. Similar is the case in regard to the birth of a child. (1) the pregnancy would take effect in its proper time (2) the womb must have the power to hold an ambryo (3) the continuity of the pregnancy without any disturbance, (4) the previous action which would induce birth as a man and (5) the effort of parents in the direction of producing a child. All the things that are seen in this world are produced by the agency of these five causes. The continuity of the existence of the earth is insured though its visible phenomena continually change. Multitudes of beings are always born, and die. The aggregate of the bodies of these beings is the earth. The view that the earth being in the form of an effect is bound to be entirely dissolved some day just as a pot, is not correct, because the earth has not exactly the same effect as a pot. A pot never involves forces of growth but the earth involves such forces, countless bodies are daily produced and destroyed. By the combination and destruction of these countless bodies, the earth remains the same. Look at a river which keeps its continuity of flow by the efflux and influx of waters. A pot is not of this nature. The earth is therefore bound to eternally exist and the phenomena of life seen on it will never disappear. It will exist everlastingly and the God is not its creator. There are many simple minded men who on seeing men, animals, earth, air, vegetables, the sun, and the moon, and the ingenious arrangement of the bones of bodies of men and animals, lids of eyes, semi-spheres of the brain, the wonderful arrangement of arteries in the body, become puzzled and when they are unable to explain the phenomena they come to believe that none but God can create these things and therefore call God the creator of the universe, but they do not know that by making this statement they bring about the destruction of God.

O, simple minded man ! if you were acquainted with 148 distinctions of 8 kinds of actions you would not have impaired the greatness of God by imputing to Him the creation of the world. Whatever acts have been attributed to God by the imagination of man are proved to be the result of actions themselves. These actions are described in brief as below :—

What action is according to the belief of the Jains, is thus explained. Just as a man having rubbed his body with oil goes about in the town and fine atoms of dust get stuck to his body by the contact of oil rubbed thereon, exactly so the inner impressions of such moral flaws as injury to living beings, falsehood, theft, sexual intercourse, extortion, anger, pride, illusion, covetousness, passion, hatred, quarrel, calumny, jealousy, scandal, like or dislike, sentiments, false utterances, sentimental grievance, which may all be considered of the nature of oil, get mixed up with the atoms of matter and constitute what is called the subtle body of desire. This body accompanies the soul indispensably from all eternity. It contains countless potentialities of merit and demerit. This body according to the belief of Jains, is called Karma ; according to the belief of the follower of Sankhya, nature; according to the Vedantis, illusion; and according to the Naiyayik and Vaisheshik, something invisible. Some divide these into past, present and future actions. Budhists call them desires or Vasnas. Thoughtless people call these actions as the work of God or nature, but no follower of any religion knows accurately the nature of these actions because in these religions there has been no all knowing sage who could accurately describe them. People falling into the net of delusion or ignorance set up by the imagination of various writers, blindly follow innumerable paths of religion. The eight kinds of actions are :—

(1) Actions that obscure knowledge, (2) Actions that obscure cognition, (3) Actions that create feelings (of pain or pleasure,) (4) Actions that bring on delusion, (5) Actions that determine period of life (Age), (6) Actions that determine the individuality (Name,) (7) Actions that determine the surroundings (Clan,) (8) Actions that inferfere with the performance or enjoyment of good things.

The first is of five kinds, the second of nine, the third of two, the fourth of 28, the fifth of 4, the sixth of 93, the seventh of 2, and the eigth of 5 kinds *i. e.* there are altogether 148 kinds which are not separately described here for fear of space.

My books entitled "The Esaimat Samiksha" (Examination of Christian faith) and the Jain Prashnottâravali (Questions and answers on Jainism) may be referred to by those desirous of further particulars regarding the characteristics of these 148 tendencies. For detailed information regarding the kinds and diversions of actions, Karma-grantha, Pancha Sangraha, Karmaprakriti Shataka and other works may be consulted. The wonderful mechanism of bodies is made by the operation of these 148 tendencies of actions. As the effects of food impart juice to the bones, muscles, eyelids, parts of brain, the general strength of the body is developed; God takes no part in this operation, but Time, nature, law of continuity, action and energy are bringing about the wonderful creation of the world. If believers in God mean by God the combination of these five essentials, then there is no objection on our part. Except these causes, there is no creator. The objection that these divisions and kinds of actions are only the figments of imagination of the Jains is absurd because the divisions are accepted by the Jains in view of their peculiar effects and can be established by argument and they have been seen directly by the eye of pure knowledge of the all-knowing and passionless sage (Tirthankar). The marvellous creation of the world cannot be proved by means of other than these causes. Sensible men should therefore accept the faith propounded by the Arhats. A passionless, all-knowing God can never be proved as the creator of the world as has already been shown. One who desires to know in detail the arguments refuting the view that God is the creator of the world may consult the following books :—

1. Sammati-tarka (सम्मति तर्क)
2. Dwâdashâsâr Nayachakra (द्वादशासार नयचक्र)
3. Syâdvâd Ratnâkar (स्याद्वाद रत्नाकर)
4. Anekânt Jayapatâkâ (अनेकान्त जयपताका)

5. Shâstra Vârtâ Samuchchai (शास्त्र वार्ता समुच्चय)
6. Syâdvâd Kalpalatâ (स्याद्वाद कल्प-लता)
7. Syâdvâd Manjari (स्याद्वाद मंजरी)
8. Syâdvâd Ratnâkarâvatârikâ (स्या-द्वाद रत्नाकरावतारिका)
9. Sûtra Kritânga (सूत्र कृतांग
10. Nandi-Sûtra नन्दी सूत्र
11. Shabdâmbhonidhi Gandhâsti-Mahâbhâshya (शब्दांभोनिधि गंधास्ती महाभाष्य)
12. Pramân Samuchchai (प्रमाण समु-च्चय)
13. Pramân Parikshâ (प्रमाण परीक्षा)
14. Prameya Mimânsâ (प्रमेय मीमांसा)
15. Apta Mimânsâ (आप्त मीमांसा)
16. Prameya Kamal Mârtanda (प्रमेय कमल मार्तंड)
17. Prameyaghan Mârtanda (प्रमेयघन मार्तंड)
18. Nyâyâvatâra (न्यायवतार)
19. Dharmasangrahni (धर्मसंग्रहणी)
20. Tattvârtha (तत्त्वार्थ)
21. Shaddarsana-Samuchchaya (षड्-दर्शन समुच्चय)

59 Q.—How has God been described in ancient scriptures ?

A.—The Jain Shastras hold that the position of Arhat and Siddha is that of God. How this position is attained, is stated as below. When a soul through a great number of births has been assiduously practising the path of virtue, rectitude and justice according to the teaching of Arhats, and practises the difficult path of twenty virtues in his last third birth aspiring to be an Arhat, it becomes fit to attain the position of a Tirthankar. In course of time such a one is born in a celestial region from where he comes down and takes his birth in a happy, prosperous, noble and good royal family. If in the former birth he has acquired by his meritorious acts a privilege to enjoy worldly pleasures then he has to enjoy the best of worldly pleasures and dominion. If he has not acquired the said privilege, he can enjoy neither worldly pleasures nor power. Such beings as are to attain the position of Arhats, are born with three kinds of knowledge i.e., Mati, Shruta and Avadhi.

He knows by his own knowledge the time when he should adopt Renunciation. If his parents are living he takes their permission to retire from the world. If they are not living he takes permission for his holy mission from his brothers or other members of the family. A year before his initiation countless celestial beings come to him and say "O Bhagvan, show the path of virtue and rectitude." A year after, he enters the path of initiation with great festivities after making bounteous gifts of gold Mohars, but he makes no one his teacher or preceptor as he is himself to be the preceptor of the three worlds. As he is full of knowledge he relinquishes all sins, and practises severest austerities. He destroys all the four kinds of actions that impede soul's progress and becomes self-enlightened. He then preaches truths that lead beyond the net of the world and reveal virtue and rectitude. Such a one is Tirthankar. The acts which help towards the attainment of birth as Tirthankar and the twenty virtues alluded to above and involved in the performance of these acts are as follows :—

The acts of reverence and devotion to the seven holy beings and their faithful service. These seven are Arhat, Siddha, Pravachana-sangha, Guru or Preceptor, Sthavir, Bahushruta, and Tapasvi (ascetic). The act of constantly contemplating in one's mind the forms of the above seven. The act of zealous observance of the virtues of right seeing and modesty. The faultless observance of the necessary acts of self-control. The act of constantly observing the Mulaguna (five great vows) and Uttarguna (purification of the body &c). The act of right thinking every hour, every minute and every second throughout life. The act of observing austerities or giving alms to holy persons. The act of observing ten kinds of vows of service. The act of promoting mental peace of the holy teachers and others. The act of acquiring fresh knowledge. The act of spreading with faith the knowledge of Truth. The act of revering the scriptures. The act of constantly following the path that has been preached by Arhats and endeavouring to one's ability to propagate the same. Some secure the ultimate attainment of Tirthankarhood by practising, out of these virtues, one, and some, two, others three and some, all the twenty. Particulars of these are given in such works as the Jnâtâ Dharmakathâ, Kalpasûtra, Avashyaka &c. A Tirthankar never desires any reward for his good acts ; his teaching is beneficial alike to a prince and a beggar, a Brahman and a Chandâl and is calculated to take one beyond the ocean of rebirth. The merits of a Tirthankar cannot adequately be described even by such high celestial beings as Indra &c. It is therefore impossible for a man of my little understanding to do them full justice. Even then something is attempted. A Tirthankar is endowed with infinite qualities—a few of which are these: Infinite pure knowledge, infinite pure vision, infinite power of action, infinite fivefold possessions, forgiveness, uncovetousness, uprightness, prideless-ness, humility, truth, self-control, selfless-ness, celebacy, compassion, benevolence, absence of hatred and passions. Equality of disposition towards friend and foe, gold and stone, woman and straw, absti-nence from flesh-food and wine and other uneatable things, immovability. He is the ocean of compassion. He is powerful, valiant, sober, courageous, fear-less, devoid of evil-speaking, unegoistic, desirous to save even those who do him ill. This is the description of the form of the Jains' God with body. When the body is discarded, he attains the position of a Siddha who dwells in his own eternal and infinite bliss. The God of the Jains has nothing to do with the creation of the world, or the task of taking incarnations, or the task of punishing or rewarding people according to their merits or demerits or sending them to heaven or hell or showing pride in his being the ruler of the world. This is in brief the description of God as believed in by the Jains. The Naiyayikas and Vaisheshikas consider Shiva to be the God who creates and destroys the world, rewards and punishes men according to their good or evil actions and sends them to heaven or hell, pervades the whole universe, takes periodical incarnations in the world to destroy the wicked and protect the good. The Buddhists believe in a God similar to that of the Jains but they believe in his incarnations in the world, the followers of the Vedas believe that whatever there is in the world is God. The followers of Nir-ishwar Sankhya School and Jaimini philosophy do not believe in God at all.

60 *Q.*—What view of God can be held according to modern science?

A.—The modern science is not opposed to the Jain scriptures; it is in harmony with them. The Arhats have ascribed infinite powers to matter. There was also a work on the subject by the name of Yoniprâbhrita Shâstra which related to the chemistry of things. What the existing ancient Jain scriptures say is in accordance with science. What has been, is and will be in this world is the result of the combination of matter and spirit. The cosmic laws that are, have been existing from all eternity by the strength of material and spiritual forces. This is why the Jains do not hold God to be the creator of the world. That God is not the creator of the world has already been established by a series of reasoning. If the forces of matter are to be considered

God, then the Jains have no objection to it. The Jain belief is not therefore opposed to the conclusion of modern science. If it is contended that all substances, all the forces inherent in them and that all the laws of the world have been created by the power of God, it is repudiated by the argument that no effects come into being without their material causes—an argument recognised valid by all learned men. Matter and spirit are therefore to be accepted eternal. When this has been conceded, the forces inherent in them will have also to be recognised as eternal. These forces manifest and destroy themselves when they get the aid of their concommittant causes such as Time, disposition, law, inter action, and mutual combination. According to the modern science the view of God as held by other religionists is found invalid.

61. Q.—In what respects do statements about God found in different religious books agree and in what do they differ?

A.—Jains, Naiyayikas, Patanjalists, Buddhists, and the followers of the Vedas hold God to be omniscient. That God is without a body is a common belief. That God is one without any beginning is the belief of the followers of Nyaya and Vaisheshika doctrines and of the Vedas. The Jains and the Buddhists hold God to be beginningless but not one. The followers of the Vedas and of the Nyaya and Vaisheshika doctrine believe God to be the creator of the universe but this is not the view of the Jains and the Buddhists. All except the Jains believe that God takes incarnations in the world, being born in the womb of a woman. Except the Jains and the Buddhists the followers of all other religions consider God to be omnipresent. The Jains too consider God to be omnipresent by reason of his faculty of knowledge and not owing to his body. God is considered to do justice and give reward or punishment to all beings by all religionists except the Jains and the Buddhists. Similar is the view as regards God's power to do what he likes. In respect to the following attributes of God, all religions hold a common view, subject to differences now and then in the meanings of these words.

The attributes are :—

Without age, without death, without birth, without measure, without impurity, without form, unthinkable, uncountable,

Brahm, Lord, infinite, immutable, Lord of the ascetics, full of knowledge, stainless, unchangeable, undecaying Supreme Lord, Supreme goal, controller, bliss, self existence, incomprehensible, knower of present, past and future, master-Lord, Lord of the Universe, immovable, unperishable, &c. &c.

62. Q.—What are the views about the existence of God in modern times ?

A.—The atheists hold that there are no such things as soul, God, merit or demerit, heaven or hell, salvation &c. except the five elements of earth, water, fire, air and space from which all other things *viz.*, soul etc., naturally evolve and dissolve. Many men believe that whatever happens in the world happens by the desire of God. It is God and God alone who creates, nourishes, and destroys. Many others believe that the world has been created by God who gives happiness of heaven or sufferings of hell to the created beings according to their good or bad actions. The Vedantists hold that whatever there is in the universe is but Brahma who manifests himself in various ways. The belief of the Jains is that when a being after having done good actions in innumerable births attains the position of a Tirthankar or Arhat in any birth, he shows to all deserving beings the way to liberation, which leads to the promulgation and performance of virtuous deeds. When a Tirthankar or Arhat shuffles off this mortal coil and attains salvation, he becomes a Siddha (the perfect) who is full of the eternal bliss of knowledge, of an eternal life of unending joys. He never does anything pertaining to the mundane affairs. These are in brief the various beliefs of people.

63 *Q.*—What is the nature of man ?

A.—It is man's nature to desire that he is highly respected and esteemed by others, that he is superior to others in prosperity riches, family, beauty, health, and physical strength, that he becomes famous in the world and that he may attain a higher position in future. By reason of tricks, anger, pride, greed, passion, jealousy, &c., man's nature is vitiated. It is by the practice of virtues that a man becomes possessed of forgiveness humility, serenity of mind, contentment, passion, hatred &c.

64 Q.—What is the superiority of man ?

A.—Man considers himself superior to all animal kingdom in wisdom.

65 Q.—In what respect is man inferior to God ?

A.—The liberated souls whether in body or without body possess pure knowledge, pure sight, infinite power, infinite happiness, immortality, birthlessness, immutability, purity, immovability, indestructability, &c.; such infinite powers are their characteristics. In the case of a man these powers remain clouded by the darkness of actions. This is the inferiority of man to God.

66 *Q.*—What position does man occupy in the creation ?

A.—Man is third in the order of these four classes of Beings *i.e.* 1. Narki, 2. Vegetable, mineral and animal kingdoms, (Tiryancha) 3. Men and 4. Angels. In respect to happiness man occupies the second position to Gods or Angels; in respect to acquisition of knowledge, performance of virtuous deeds, attainment of liberation and attainment of the position of God, man occupies the first position. He holds the same position in respect to doing evil.

67 *Q.*—What powers has soul to become man ? Has he power to become immortal or God ?

A.—Soul has the following powers to become man.

1. The softening down of delusion and passion into a mild form.
2. Good thoughts.
3. Manifestation of passion momentarily only.

4. Indiscrimination between right and wrong.

5. Propensity towards charity, without much desire for name or fame.

6. Excessive love of offering charity according to one's disposition.

7. Forgiveness, humility, pridelessness, compassion, purity, veracity. Desire for the reward of worship and other wordly desires.

Although we have already mentioned these powers in connection with the faculties of actions, we have neverthless given a brief account of them here. Soul has also powers to become God. But these powers never manifest themselves until it has been purged of its eighteen defects.

The eighteen defects are these.

1. Obstruction to unstinted distribution of charity.

2. Obstruction to unstinted possessions.

3. do. do. powers.

4. Obtruction to unstinted new enjoyments such as flowers, garlands &c.

5. Obstruction to unstinted daily enjoyments such as woman, apparells &c.

On the extinction of these five defects five powers of men come into manifestation. Just as the eye attains keen sight by the removal of eye diseases, so these powers manifest themselves in man on the disappearance of these five defects. He who has not these five powers is not fit to become God. The sixth defect is laughter. Laughter is excited by seeing or hearing or remembering something extra ordinary and laughter arises from the tendency to do such acts as bind. Both these causes are not found in Arhat. The Lord is all knowing and all seeing. There is nothing outside the limit of his knowledge by seeing, hearing, remembering which he may feel surprised. Therefore there is no laughter in Him. As regards binding acts He has none of them. He is not therefore contaminated by the defect of laughter because he who laughs must not be all knowing, all seeing, and free from the influences of action. The seventh defect is earthly love whch is not in God. He who has love must be attracted towards charming sound, beauty, dainty dishes, fragrant smells, delicate touch, &c. He who is attracted must have desire and he who has desire must be aggrieved on its non-realization. The eighth defect is aversion or hatred. He who is possessed of hatred against any person or things would not be happy because of the feeling or hatred. This cannot be said of the blessed Arhat. The ninth defect is fear. He who has not dispelled his own fear, how can he be blessed Arhat. The tenth defect is disgust which arises at the sight of unclean things. As God's knowledge is universal He must be extremely unhappy if He were possessed of the feeling of disgust. Therefore this too is not a part of the qualifications of the Lord. The eleventh defect is sorrow. He who has sorrow cannot be God. The twelvth defect is lust. He who is lustful and indulges in the sexual pleasures of women can never be called God by any sensible man. The thirteenth defect is falsehood which leads to darkness and this cannot be attributed to God. The fourteenth defect is ignorance. He who is full of ignorance can never be all-knowing God. The fifteenth defect is sleep. He who sleeps has a gap in knowledge. The blessed Arhat is all-knowing, so He is beyond sleep. The sixteenth defect is desire. He who is full of desire cannot be Arhat. The seventeenth and eighteenth defects are passion and anger. He who has passion and anger cannot be mediator. Such a man suffers from anger, pride, illusion and delusion. On the other hand the Lord is passionless, equally disposed towards friends and foe, having an equal measure of consideration for all beings. He makes none either happy or miserable. If He makes other happy or miserable, He cannot be passionless and full of compassion. For these reasons the blessed Arhat cannot have passion and hatred.

One who has any of these eighteen defects cannot be Arhat, because He is entirely free from them. Take an instance of a well polished diamond and a raw diamond that is still in mine. Although the diamond that is embedded in the mine is not bright yet it possesses all the qualities of a genuine diamond ; when it will be dressed and polished it will be considered as one of the brightest jewels. Similarly the soul has powers to become God but owing to the impurities of eight kinds of actions that have accumulated in the course of ages, these powers have not become manifest. The soul that will be brightened by the instructions of a teacher subject to five attendant causes such as time &c, its devine powers will become manifest and that man will become a God. God is not any particular man; the innumerable souls that have attained liberation in the course of immemorable ages or reached the position of Siddhas or will reach it in future have and will become God. Just as this world is eternal by reason of its unceasing continuity so the Siddhahood is also eternal. Souls have been attaining liberation from time immemorial. If you entertain a doubt that since souls have been attaining liberation from time immemorial, than a time would come when all souls have attained liberation and the worlds will be depleted of all souls. This is not right. Things which are limited in calculation will have an end but things which are unlimited in name and form will never have an end, for example, the earth and the sky. If you measure both these objects you will come to the end of the earth because it is limited but you will never come to the end of the sky because it is unlimited. Similarly the number of the souls in the world is unlimited and therefore there will be no end of the number of the souls even if they went in salvation from eternity to eternity. If you say that the number of the souls must be calculable in the unlimited knowledge of God, because it cannot be unlimited knowledge if it could not count them, the answer is that one who has unlimited knowledge views unlimited things as unlimited and the limited ones as limited. For instance, the sky is unlimited; it is similarly regarded by God. If you do not accept this explanation then whatever view of God you advance will also have this fallacy. The believers in God hold God to be beginningless and endless. Does God see His own beginning or end or no? If He sees them, then the worth of God is proved and it is also proved that there was no God before His birth. If God sees His own end then it is also possible that He would die. If you say that God does not see His beginning and end simply because God has no beginning or end, then on your own statement you will find that the knowledge of God is limited because He cannot see His beginning or end. O, Dear, the number of the souls and the measurement of the sky are equally unlimited and therefore the Lord too does not see their end. He sees the absence of that which is not and the presence of that which is.

This has been explained because it has a bearing on the subject.

68. Q.—What are the views about future life of the followers of other religions ?

A. The soul is considered to be beginningless by many men. According to this belief the soul having given up its gross body in the past assumes a variety of new bodies according to its good or bad actions. The future life of soul is its giving up body in one life and assuming a new body in the next. According as the present birth of a soul is determined by its past life so will its future life be determined by the actions of present life and those of the preceding lives. When all the actions have extinguished in a life, then there will be no more future life. Those who believe that the soul is not beginningless but one created by the God are wrong because we have already discussed as to the ability of God in such matters. Nothing can be produced in the world without a material cause, therefore, the Jains, the Buddhists, the followers of the Vedâs, Nyâya, Vaisheshika and Mimânsâ philosophies believe that the next birth of man is determined by the actions of his past life. Many others believe that the future form will be the same as in the present life *i. e.*, a man will be reborn a man, a woman a woman, an animal an animal and so on and so forth. This belief is also according to the Vedas but it is not right, because it is seen in the world that if a corn rubbed with linsed oil is sown in the earth it will produce several kinds of grain. Similarly there are many plants and vegetables which can be produced by the combination of many other things as described in Ayurveda. In the Jaina Shâstrâs many instances are given where the combination of several things can produce a certain species of life, for instance a serpant, or a diamond, gold &c. The above statement is also borne out by the conclusions of the modern science. It is consequently not established that an effect will be of the same form as its cause.

This subject is further discussed in the Visheshâvashyaka Sûtras. Some hold that a lion whose nature is to kill animals will be reborn a greater criminal. In his next birth he will be born a still greater criminal. In this manner he will get worse and still worse and will thus have no opportunity to be born as a man. The answer to this argument is that according to the views of the Jaina Shastras such as Pragyapanâ, Bhagavati &c. man of all the forms of life can assume innumerable births according to his good or bad deeds. The action that is uppermost in one life determines the birth of a man in his next life. There is no established rule that all the previous actions good or bad will immediately be attended by their corresponding results for example, a thief who commits theft sometimes gets an immediate punishment and sometimes after a long time and sometimes not at all in this life. Similarly some men reap the consequence of good or bad actions immediately, some later on in life, some in next life and others in remote lives to come. These actions are of various and complicated forms and are fully described in such works as Shat Karmagranth, Pancha-Sangraha, Karmaprakriti and others. The study of these works will bear out the truth of my statement.

The main conclusion is that according to their actions, virtuous or wicked, all beings will be reborn in their next lives. Now as regards the Chârvâkâs or the atheists who consider that life is the product of 4 elements and who do not believe in the past or future life nor in the existence of heaven or hell &c , I proceed to repudiate their doctrine as given in the commentry on Nandi sûtras. The Chârvâkâs or the atheists say that since there is no soul there is no meaning in the mutual quarrels of religionists over it. They further say that there being no soul the followers of Jainism, Buddhism, Sânkhya, Naiyâyika, Vaisheshika and Jaimini philosophies i. e. six philosophies simply lead man to confusion and perplexity and make them give up their enjoyments.

In fact there is no soul and therefore their creed is the best. If there is a soul, what proof is there of its existence? The answer to this argument is that soul is proved by the self consciousness of the man.

The consciousness of man is not the result of any material forces. If it is so then the firmness such as there is in the earth ought to always prevail everywhere, but this is not the case, because we do not find any consciousness in substance such as iron, dead bodies &c.

62. Q.—In stone etc. and also in a dead body there is life but it is merely in the form of a force and hence it is invisible.

A. This statement of yours is not correct because it involves the non-solution of two difficulties. Is that force antagonistic to life or is it life itself? If you say that it is antagonistic to life, then it is not right to say that life is in the form of a force in as much as without the existence of a garment what is in the form of garment is only an earthen jar.

If you take the second point, that force is life itself ; then the question arises as to the cause of its invisibility. If you say that it is not visible on account of a cover, it is not right to say so because a cover is another name for obstruction. Then the question arises whether that obstruction is the non-existence of the proposed change, or is another form of change or is something other than elementals. It is not the non-existence of the proposed change, because it being light it has no force of obstruction. If it is heavy it would become a form of feeling and so apart from earth etc.

The *Bhutas* such as earth etc. serve as manifestations of *chaitanya* and are not obstructions. Hence obstructibility is not proved. If you say that it is another form of the change it is also wrong to say so, because it being of the nature of elemental is the manifestator of life like elementals and not its obstruction.

If you say that it is something quite distinct from elements, that is equally wrong to say because in believing it to be quite distinct from elementals the destruction of the number of the elements would be the result. It is also to be noticed whether life is the attribute of each particular element or of all elements combined. It is not the attribute of each particular element separately, because it is not so visible. · Every atom does not appear to be endowed with consciousness. If it is in each atom then a man would have a collection of a thousand consciousness of a different kind and it would not bear a single form. But apparently it bears a single form.

viz, I see and I do.

Thus the whole body appears to be owned by one. If you believe in the attribute of a collective body it is false as it is not present in each individual atom. What is untrue from each particular point of view cannot be true collectively, for instance, the existence of oil in the individual atoms of sand.

If you say that every ingredient of wine does not possess the energy of wine and that a collection thereof does possess such a power, and that same is the case with life and that there is no fallacy in such a belief, than I would say that it is not right to say so, because every ingredient of wine possesses sweetness etc. conducive of the energy of wine. The sugar cane juice from the flowers of *dhatki* becomes intoxicating to a small extent. But life does not similarly appear in elementals. Consequently it cannot exist in a combination of elements. If what is non-existent in any separate form becomes existent in the combination of such forms, then such combinations can achieve all. There is another thing to be taken into consideration. If you believe life to be an attribute, you should necessarily believe the attribute and its subject to be identical. If you do not believe them to be identical, then it is possible to consider water and hardness as subject and attribute which is not the case. It is not right to say that elementals are subjects, in as much as they are antagonistic to chaitanya. For instance attribute of consciousness is knowledge and it is formless but an elemental is of quite a distinct form. How can the relation of subject and attribute be possible? Nor is life the cause of elementals. It being quite distinct cannot bear the relation of cause and effect. It is also remarkable that if an element be the cause of life the whole world would be full of living beings. If you say that the whole world is not full of living beings on account of absence of the transformation of a real existance then the question arises why does not the transformation of the real existence appear every where. The phenomenon of the transformed elementals can at the best be proved only an instrumental cause and it being so, how can it be proved that it is manifest in one place and not manifest in another. What is the form of that transformed reality? If you say that its form is hardness, then how weevils etc. become born in wood and similar substance. It would show that life exists even where there is hardness. This is not tenable in all cases. There are exceptional cases. Even without any presence of hardness, such creatures as spring from perspiration exist.

Another point is that animals of the same species are of different colours and sizes. Animals that execrete dung are some black, some yellowish, and so on and their sizes also differ. If elementals are instrumental cause of life, then all animals of the same species ought to have the same colour and size but this is not the case. Therefore it will have to be accepted that it is only the souls which take forms conformable to their actions. If you contend that if there is a soul, why is it not seen when transmigrating. It appears in consciousness only in a body, and when the body is destroyed it is not perceptible. Does it not prove that there is no soul? It is per ceptible only in tbe body as consciousness which is the product of the body upon which it depends for its existence. It does not exist independently and is like a picture on the wall, which disappears with the destruction of the wall nor can be transferred to another wall. Similarly is the case with consciousness. This argument is fallacious. The soul is formless and the internal body is very subtle and it is hence that the soul though migrating with its subtle kârman body is not seen. It can be perceived only by its characteristics. A creature though just born has an idea of individuality. It runs away at the sight of its enemy. The individuality is determined by its previous tendencies. So long as the good or evil of a thing is not perceived it does not abstract or repel any one.

The propensities which we see at the birth of a creature are the result of the tendencies of the past life. The transmigration of soul is therefore proved.

How is the knowledge of soul to be arrived at by an inference when its movements are not visibly seen.

Your statement is not correct. The

direct evidence does not reach the subject of inference. The learned accept the application of direct evidence to objects which are of the same nature.

The illustration of a wall-picture which you gave is also inapplicable. The picture is lifeless, the act of going is not natural, the soul is conscious and migrates by the force of its actions. These being the discrepancies, how does your illustration apply to the subject to be explained. Just as Devdutta having dwelt in a village for a time leaves it and removes to another village, so the soul having given up a body in a particular region, migrates to another region and assumes a different body. Your statement about the sensation being the product of body is not correct. It may be that perceptions such as we have through our senses such as eyes &c are partly due to the body owing to their concern with the organs of senses but it is absolutely wrong to contend that the mental knowledge springs from the body. Does the mental knowledge spring from the body in the form of a sense-organ or without such a form, or does it spring from such outward bodily appertances as hair, nails &c. The first question is not right. If it springs in the form of a sense-organ, its knowledge ought to be limited to the present perceptions only because the perceptions of the sense-organs limit themselves only to the present phenomena. On this assumption the mental knowledge would limit itself only to the present phenomena as the sense-organs. It is only when the eye sees a form that it forms its idea, not at any other time. The presence of the form is then the cause of its perception. The mental knowledge does not depend upon the presence of a form and it is not therefore limited to any particular time. The same argument applies in the case of other sense-organs. The mental knowledge does not therefore depend upon the phenomena of any particular time. If it does not spring in the form of a sense-organ, the position is still faulty for it is unconscious. As regards the hair, nails &c being the cause of mental knowledge it would suffice to say that since they never appear affected by mental thoughts they can never be the said cause. If the mental knowledge is bound by the hair, nails &c it is capable of being totally destroyed by their removal. If the hair, nails &c. are hurt, the mental knowledge should also receive a corresponding hurt but this is not the case ; therefore this third argument also falls to the ground.

Moreover subtility of sense, logical distinctions and acuteness of memory are features of mental knowledge but these are cultivated by constant practice. The same books when studied frequently and closely show deeper and deeper meanings and the acuteness of memory is also cultivated. In this manner when one book is studied and its meaning thoroughly grasped and the memory sharpened, it leads to an easy understanding of other books and the memory is developed. Such mental phenomena are often seen which are acquired by constant practice. Sometimes such mental characteristics are seen natural and not acquired by practice but practice and exercise are the chief elements. Cause and effect move in unison. Causes though invisible certainly exist as in the case of pilgrimage of soul to another world. Although the body is liable to destruction and extinction it can nevertheless help towards the progress of knowledge. With the destruction of the body, knowledge is not extinguished. Look at the fire and the pot when the fire ceases to burn the pot is not destroyed. Similar is the case with gold and fire. When the body is destroyed, knowledge no doubt receives some shock but is not radically destroyed. If you accept that knowledge is destroyed with the body, then with the burning up of the body in the cremation ground all knowledge will have extinguished. Can it be explained why does it not appear in a dead body which has not yet been burned.

If you say that Prân and Apân are also causes of knowledge which ceases when these causes do not exist. This position is not correct. Prân and Apân cannot be the causes of knowledge. It is the knowledge which brings them into action. Prân and Apân for their motions depend upon the meagreness or intensity of the desire of a man.

If the body is the cause of the Prân and Apân and Prân and Apán the cause of knowledge, then the action of Prân and Apân will not be at the command of one's desire. If Prân and Apân are the causes of knowledge then the degrees of intensity will produce corresponding proportions of knowledge because it is commonly established that an effect varies with its cause in its extent or dgree. For example a pot will be large or small according to the large or small quantity of the earth employed to make it. If this is not the case then there is no relation of cause and effect. You are not unaware that your knowledge does not increase or decrease with the increase or decrease of the Prân or Apân. On the other hand the contrary is the case as may be seen at the time of the death of a man when the Prân and Apân are so much in play while the knowledge or consciousness is reduced to a zero. If you say that the increase of the Prân and Apân at the time of death is due to the humours of the wind and biliousness &c. which vitiate the body and do not allow consciousnes to come into play. This statement is incorrect. If this is so a dead man ought to be alive because after the death the humours of the wind and biliousness &c. disappear and the body is also free from fever and other diseases and the absence of these ailments means health. Since the body is healthy in such a state it ought to be alive. If this is not so then the body is not the cause of consciousness, and it has not any relation of cause and effect with the mind. If a dead man were to get alive we would believe the body to be the cause of consciousness.

70\. Q.—Your argument about a dead man getting alive is improper. Although the ailments which vitiate the body at the time of death disappear, the vitiating effect which they create in the body do not disappear just as the effect caused by fire in the wood never disappears although the fire extinguishes.

A.—This is not right. Changes are of 2 kinds. One kind of change altogether disappears and the other does not. The second kind of change is caused by the fire in the wood when it is burnt and the first kind of change is caused by it, in the gold when it is burnt. The humours of wind &c. are such as disappear according to the science of medicine. If they do not disappear then the science of medicine is wrong. Moreover it cannot be that ailments which disappear while the man is alive do not disappear when he is dead. A change cannot have two aspects in the same place.

71\. Q—Diseases are of two kinds—curable and incurable. The curable diseases are removed by treatment but the incurable diseases never disappear. Does it not show that there are two aspects of diseases ?

A.—This too is not right. According to you there can be no incurable disease. The incurability of the disease means the extinction of life. During an ordinary disease a man sometimes dies by the quackery of a physician and sometimes he does not die. The diseases which are the result of evil actions of man are not cured by any medicines. Both these diseases are to be found only in the religions of those who believe in the teachings of the Lord but not in the religion of those like you who believe only in the elements. Sometimes a medicine is efficacious in curing the effects of ailments but sometime in the absence of a physician an ordinary disease becomes incurable. Owing to the absence of a physician and medicine, a disease is aggravated and ends only in the death of a man. Sometimes a man suddenly dies as soon as his ailments disappear and sometimes a man does not die though seriously afflicted with virulent diseases.

These things can have no place in your creed. According to our doctrine, a man lives his fixed age though afflicted with serious diseases but when his fixed age has reached its limit he dies though there are no diseases ailing him. The body is not therefore the cause of consciousness. There is another point. Do you believe the body to be a concommitant or material couse of consciousness or knowledge? If you believe in the former, we too consider the body to be the means of death and to some extent the cause of knowledge. If you believe in the latter, the position is wrong. A material cause is that which communicates its changes to its effects just as the earth and the pot. When the body is affected, the sense of feeling is not affected. On the other hand, the mind is affected a good deal by fear, anxiety, grief &c even when the body is all right. The body is not therefore the material cause of the sense of feeling.

This statement also disposes of the argument that the life of the parents is the material cause of the life of the child. When the parents are affected by ailments, the children are not similarly affected. But a material cause always follows its effect and cannot be separated from it just as the earth and the pot. If the life of the parents is inseparable from the life of the child, the latter's life should have a similar relation. This will show that the qualities or effects of elementals are not feelings. It also proves that there is a soul. Further information regarding the creed of the Chârvâkâs is to be found in such works as Sanmati-tarka, Syâdvâdaratnâkara &c.

72. Q.—What do the old Shâstrâs say with regard to the social and friendly dealings of human beings among themselves ?

A.—A man should have friendly feelings towards human beings, do good to them, assist them in trouble, preach true Law (truth) if he knows, should not take pride in his 'high' caste, should be hospitable to them by giving food etc.

73. Q.—What is in fact the relation of man with God ?

A.—The relation is that of an instructor and the instructed.

74 Q.—What should man do for God ?

A.—God does not want anything, but devoted men should in order to wipe off their evil actions, worship God by installing his image of the form such as He had when He attained liberation while living in the world, invoke God in that idol by their feeling of devotion, and attributing His nature to it. Although the idol is not God, yet through that idol, God is worshipped. Thus an idol becomes a sort of memorial of the God. All the different religionists say that their respective sacred books are the words of God. The Christian, Mahommadens and Brahmins etc. say so with regard to their Bible, Kurân and Vedâs etc. respectively. The Christians take oath by taking the Bible in their hands or holding it over their heads. The Musalmans respect their Kurân very much. As a matter of fact these books are nothing else than paper and ink. But in order to recollect the knowledge of God, the *murti* (form) of letters is made by persons with their own hands and they are respected. As people understand the knowledge of God with the help of those letters which have been written by them, similarly with the help of idols the form of God who attained liberation while living in the world is apprehended.

The maps of countries are drawn on small and large sized papers and the teachers point to their pupils in those maps saying, "Look here, this is Italy, this is Russia, this is America, this is India etc." The pupils do not believe that the very place upon which their teacher kept a finger is Italy or Russia etc. But these maps help them to understand the real countries Italy, Russia etc. Similarly we also do not believe that an idol is really the God, but that these idols help us in understanding God the preacher of truth. For this reason we must believe in (the efficacy of) the idols of God. Those who do not believe in the idols of God, must not respect their religious books, nor should they take oath on them. The belief in idols includes belief in books. For this reason, we must invoke God through aforesaid idols, remember His virtues, pronounce that He is free from 18 defects and is undefiled. If you believe in this way, then it is not an idol but God Himself. Taking God himself to be present there and knowing that He is from eternity the preacher of true righteousness (Dharma) and the doer of the greatest good, we must worship Him in accordance with the forms fixed for it. There are different forms of worship. I give here only a very brief account of a particular form of worship called *ashta-prakâri pûjâ* or eightfold devotion.

1. First, wash the image of God with water full of this thought "O God Arhat ! as I

remove the dirt caused by dust etc, by means of water and produce a cooling effect, your worship may also remove the dirt of all my actions *Karmâs* and the removal thereof make manifest the real nature which is *shital* (cool)."

2. Then prepare a mixture of sandal wood, safron and camphor by grinding them and smear it over the idol with a prayer in your mind "O Bhagwân ! as this smearing removes bad smell, your worship may remove also my bad *vâsnâ* (desire) which I hold from eternity."

3. Then take the best kinds of flowers giving good smell and make an offering thereof before God contemplating in your mind "O Lord ! these flowers are the arrows of *Kâmadeva* (cupid), I make an offering thereof before you in order that I may for ever be liberated from the sufferings of *Kâmadeva* (passionate desire, cupid)."

4. Then take fragrant *dhûp* (incense) and keep it upon fire so that the vapour may issue, saying in your mind, "O God ! as

this incense is burning in fire, all my vices may also be annihilated by *bhakti* (worship) and as the vapours of incense are going upward, similarly I may also attain higher life."

5. Then light a lamp with *ghi* (of cow's milk) and keep it before God saying in your mind "O Lord ! as lamp-light removes darkness, in consequence of your worship, the lamp of perfect and pure knowledge may become lighted in my heart so that the darkness of ignorance may be removed."

6. Then take good rice and keep it before God contemplating that the worship with rice may confer upon you eternal happiness.

7. Take all sorts of good *pakwân* (Cooked food) in a tray and keep it before God saying in your mind "O God ! I have been eating it from eternity, now I make an offering of the whole of it to you so that I may never feel hungry."

8. Take good fruits and put them before God thinking in your mind, "O God! in consequence of your worship I may bear the fruit of *mukti* (highest stage of attainment)."

After performing the worship with the aforesaid *dravya* (articles), one should make *chaitya-vandana* (a bow to all the Jain temples repeating God's virtues) i. e. eulogise God by mentioning his virtues in the way of saluting Him. He should praise His name in so far as is in his power to do, spread his teaching (Dharma) and improve himself by going on pilgrimage and performing *rathayâtrâ* (taking the image of God in a chariot along with a procession) and promulgate the Dharma preached by Him in different countires. These are some of the ways in which the devout should worship God.

75. Q.—Does man in reality possess or not, the attributes of Dharma ?

A.—Yes, he does possess those attributes in reality in as much as Dharma (essential quality) conveys only the idea of Dharma (one who makes Dharma) as sweetness in *misri* (a kind of sweet). The very term Dharma proves itself the connection of Dharma and Dharmi.

76. Q.—How does the connection of man with God appear in this world what is it in reality ?

A.—Many people believe that God is their father. For this reason they believe that the connection between God and man is that of father and son. Many believe that God is their creator and that they are entirely in His mind, that He makes them do what He wills and that man can not do anything. Some say that this world is the plaything of God and that He is seeing this fun. Some say that God has created this universe and that He maintains it. Some believe that God makes them suffer the consequences of their actions. The Jains say that this universe is eternal, that God is our guide and saves us from evil path. These are some of the different beliefs.

77 Q.—What is the highest achievement of Dharma and what are the characteristics of Dharma ?

A.—The highest achievement of Dharma consists in lifting man ultimately to the highest position of a Siddha or God after it has extinguished his various physical and mental afflictions consequent upon birth and death. The characteristics of Dharmi are ten :—

(1) human life, (2) birth in a civilized country, (3) noble family, (4) long life, (5) possession of complete five senses, (6) wisdom, (7) good health, (8) contact of a true teacher, (9) hearing of the noble teaching preached by God free from eighteen faults, and (10) belief in the above said teaching and acting thereupon.

78 Q.—What are the ways of worship and observance of Dharma according to different religions ?

A.—The worship according to Jains has already been described above in connection with the eightfold mode of worship. There are two modes of Dharma or duty — the duty of a householder and that of a recluse. First — take the duty of a house holder.

A householder ought always to worship God three times a day, ought not to injure visible animate objects, to speak falsehood, to commit serious theft, and to have sexual intercourse with another's wife, ought to limit a desire for possession, regulate his going abroad, avoid taking 22 kinds of non-eatables such as meat, strong drink etc and 32 kinds of *anantkaya*, ought to avoid (so far as practicable) 15 forms of bad business and 4 kinds of undesirable injuries, ought to observe devotion for an hour putting on clean clothes, whenever he gets an opportunity to do so, and give up all kinds of vicious acts, remember the qualifications of *panch parmeshti*, acquire education, observe 14 vows every day, abstaining from indulging in 4 things viz. (1) taking food, (2) beautifying body, (3) sexual intercourse and (4) business, on the two 8th, one 5th, 15th and 30th days of a month etc. ought to lead the life of a sâdhu (recluse) by doing Dharma, meditating, remembering the qualifications of *panchpermeshti* etc. for 24 hours, *i. e.*, perform what is called *poshad karma.* He ought to give alms to a deserving person, to the needy and also to the persons in trouble, carry on business according to rules of justice. This is a short description of the mode of a householder's life according to Jainism. Secondly I briefly deal with the duty of a recluse.

A *sâdhu*—a recluse ought not to injure any life, ought not to speak any kind of falsehood, ought not to commit any kind of theft, ought not to indulge in any kind of sexual intercourse, and ought not to have a desire for any thing. He should entirely abstain from these five things. He ought not to stay anywhere considering it to be his own place, ought to take in begging *madhukari bhikshâ* free from 42 defects, ought to regard a friend and an enemy, gold and stone, woman and grass equally, he should neither love nor hate anything. He ought to be prepared to bear 22 kinds of afflictions and 16 troubles which befall him. He ought to desire neither life nor fear death. He ought to check the five sexual desires. He ought to be free from anger, pride, attachment, avarice. He ought to observe 18000 characteristics of *shilanga* (chastity) This is the mode in which a monk ought to lead his life.

The other religions describe many methods which are the figments of fancies; we need not therefore describe them.

79 Q.—What are the true and real distinguishing marks of a Dharmic (pious) life and worldly life ?

A.—The true and real marks of worldly life are as follows :—

One who earns money by lawful means, admires a good act, marries in the family of a man of a different *gotra* equal to him in position, character etc, fears vicious acts, does not do anything against the fashion of his country, does not speak ill of any one, more particularly does not inhabit in too public or too private a place, lives in the neighbourhood of a good person, does not live in the house which has several passages for egress and ingress, lives in the company of a religious man, serves his parents, does not live at a place which is the source of dispute, does not do that work which is considered bad by the public, spends according to his income, lives up to his means, is possessed of the eight attributes of intelligence, always bears dharma, does not take food again until the previous food has been digested, eats contentedly at the proper time, practises virtue and has recourse to wordly pleasure and business in a way not detrimental to any of these three, supplies according to his means food, clothes etc to a holy man or a poor man who comes to his house, does not go against the propriety of time and place, does every work to the best of his ability, worships, serves one who follows great vows and is a learned man, maintains those who deserve support, is a prudent and farsighted man who knows much and is always grateful to him who has done anything for him, is loved by all, is submissive, merciful, is of agreeable nature, is doing good to others, is resolute in giving up the company of 6 inner enemies viz, passion, anger, avarice, pride, *mada* and joy, controls the contact of the senses with their objects. One who observes the aforesaid 35 things is said to truly possess all the attributes of a householder. The attributes of a Dharmic person have already been described under the head of duties of householder and saint.

80 Q.—What power does the soul of human being possess to get a high position ?

A.—The high positions are two, one secular and the other spiritual. The secular position are such as of Indra, Chakravarti, Vasudeva, Baldeva, Mandlik Raja etc. The doing of the aforesaid 35 things enable one to attain this position.

The powers in soul to attain the spiritual position viz that of God, are the ways in which a recluse should lead his life.

81 Q.—What are such acts of Dharma as are beyond controversy ?

A.—No believer doubts in the goodness of such things as showing mercy towards living beings, truth speaking, non-stealing, abstinence from adultery, forgiving, charitable temper, kind heartedness, contentment, doing good to other etc.

82 Q.—Is it essential to study the sacred books of different religions ?

A.—The reason why it is necessary to study the sacred books of different religions is that one who does so impartially and without any prejudice would find out the real truth.

83 Q.—What are the rules and conditions governing such a study ?

A.—Before you study a sacred book, you must see that its author is free from 18 faults, that there are no contradictions in his statements, that whatever he says is not contrary to what is visible in the world by direct proof and that it stands the three tests.

You must believe in all the contents of the book which like gold stands these tests. The tests are these. 1st rub the gold over *Kasauti* (test—stone), 2nd by examining it by boring it and 3rd by making it red hot in fire. The price of gold which stands these three tests is fit to be accepted. Similarly the sacred book which prohibits the doing of all sinful acts and dictates the ways of acting upon what is contrary to sinful acts i. e. a book which for the purpose of liberation prohibits the doing of sinful acts and dictates the way of acting upon what is contrary to them is called by Tirthankar Bhagwân a *Kash Shudha Shastra.* Thus a book which for the purpose of *mukti* dictates observance of meditation, study, mercy, truth *shil* (chastity, morality, good conduct), contentment etc, all combined and prohibits doing injury to living being, speaking false hood, committing theft, keeping wife, having possessions, anger, arrogance, *Mâyâ* (illusion), avarice, etc, is a *Kash shudha Shâstra.* The Shâstra which deals with *arth* (wealth), *kâm* (passion) combined, and is full of stories and shows the ways to *mokshha* in a secondary way is not *kash shudha shâstra.* The shâstra which deals with all the constructive and destructive methods of worship and conduct is called a *chheda shudha shâstra.* A saint should take care of the living beings even when he answers the calls of nature. It is most proper to take care of living beings in doing every *dhârmic* act.

The *shâstra* which prohibits the doing of an act for one purpose and dictates its doing for another purpose cannot be called *chhed* (*shudhi-shâstra*). For instance the Vedas which when dealing with the question of liberation prohibits injury to living beings and when dealing with the question of worldly possession sanction such an injury. The *shâstra* which is tested by the fire of the real qualities of things as described and tested from all the points of views and is found to be free from the black spots of superstition is called a *tâp shuddhi shâstra.* The *shâstra* which describes the attributes of things from a single point of view, is not called *tâp shuddhi shâstra.* The aforesaid tests relate to the shâshtras. It is also a necessary condition that the author of the true *shâstra* must be faultless and omniscient.

84 Q.—What traditions are there on the subject and what is their present form ?

A.—Shuk alias Parivrâjak, son of Vyâsaji, ascertained the real truth from muni Thâvachchaputra, desciple of Lord Arishtnemi and accepted the true *dharmâ.* It is so described in Sri Gnâtâ Sûtra. The Nirâvalikâ Sûtra says that Somal Brahman learned 14 sciences (4 Vedas, 6 angâs, *dharma mimânsâ*, Tarka or Mâyâ, and the Purâna) and after enquiries accepted the householder's duties *grahasth dhar-*

ma. The Bhagavati Sûtra says that Somal Brahman learned 14 sciences and after enquiring about the elements accepted the Jaina religion. Shayyambhava Bhat, the author of the Dasha-Vaikâlika Sutra gave up Mimânsak religion and became the desciple of Muni Prabhava Swami. The following 11 Brahmans (1) Indra Bhuti, (2) Agni Bhuti, (3) Vayu Bhuti, (4) Wyakt Swami, (5) Sudharmâ, (6) Mandit Putra, (7) Maurya Putra, (8) Akampita, (9) Achal Bhrâtâ, (10) Metarya and (11) Prabhãs along with the 4400 desciples—all learned in 14 sciences—ascertaining the truths, took *Diksha* (initiation) from the venerable Lord Mahâvira the 24th Tirthankara and became his desciples.

85 Q.—What effects have the dead religions of the world upon mankind at present ?

A.—The Jaina, Veda or Mimânsak, Naiyâyik, Sânkhya, Pâtanjal and Buddha religions are counted among the oldest religions of India. Now all the above religions excepting Buddhism have their existence in

India. All of these excepting Jainism are almost dying. In other countries where the Dharma of the Karma-Kândi Mimânsakâs has disappeared, its effect is that people make sacrifices by killing animals and inorder to please God make offerings of skin, flesh, and blood by killing bullocks etc. as is described in Tauret and Quran etc. Also the book named Iliad says in its account of war that Hector and other great warriors made sacrifices to gods by killing different kinds of animals. All this appears to be the remnant of Mimânsak religion. The *sufism* among Mohammedans appears to be the relic of Vedantism. In India some people of the Brahman caste etc have given up *Hinsak-yagn* and avoid flesh eating and drinking etc ; this appears to be the after-effect of Jainism and Buddhism. In other countries also the existence of virtuous acts such as mercy etc appears to be the remnant of Jainism and Buddhism.

86 Q.—What position does God of the whole universe hold according to every religion

in human progress ? God is just. According to every religion, God is the Lord of the whole universe. Then how is it that notwithstanding the differences in human progress in different people in different countries, there is no contradiction among them with regard to God's nature of being just. How do the different religions account for God on this point.

A.—All the different religions believe that God is just and this is true because God naturally possess the quality of *nyaya-shilatâ* (being just). But the belief of the people that God like Government officials administers justice to all the living beings is against the *shâstrâs* of the Jain religion and is also against logical conclusions. For instance a Baniya (trader) possess 1000 gold mohurs and for that reason he feels himself very happy. Then a thief comes and takes away all those mohurs. On the Baniya's making a protest the thief wounds his body by a sword. Thereupon the Baniya keeps quiet and the thief goes away with the money and feels himself very happy. Now supposing that the Baniya was feeling very happy by reason of possessing 1000 gold mohurs, that this was given to him by just God in consequence of his doing good actions, that in consequence of his doing sinful acts God punished him in this way that the thief took away gold mohurs and wounded the Baniya by a sword. But the question arises whether God made him suffer the consequences with or without a *nimit* (means). He cannot be said to suffer the consequences without any *nimit* because in the Baniya suffering the consequences of his bad actions the thief and sword etc were the *nimit*. Now if it be taken for granted that God puts all causes into motion, then God would be proved to cause others to do evil acts such as theft etc. If God does not put *nimits* into motion then God cannot be proved to be just and the giver of reward and punishment. If without peoples' doing good or bad acts, God gives reward or punishment to them or creates many in royal family, healthy in life, in very comfortable circumstances, satisfies all desires etc, creates some miserable from pregnancy during the whole life, mentally and physically in pain, hungry, suffering from chronic diseases ; no intelligent, man would call such God to be just, merciful, impartial, having an equal eye upon all. If God gives comfort or pain to all living beings according to their good or bad actions, then this would be proved to be eternal and God would be proved to be unjust and the faults such as theft, immorality, speaking falsehood etc would be imputed to Him.

87 Q.—You should put to God Himself the question of creation of the universe as to how and wherefrom He created the universe and why did He create happy and miserable lives ?

A.—If God were to say to us that He created the universe and that He created happy and miserable lives not consequent upon their good and bad actions, then we would put the question to Him. But God never tells us those things. Hence we put these questions to you. Consequently God is not the administrator of justice (to the living beings) in the universe, nor does He make the human beings high or low, wealthy or destitute, happy or miserable, rich or poor, educated or ignorant, beautiful or ugly. For instance a man is travelling and while on his way a brick or a piece of stone or wood etc. falls down from a house upon his head in consequence of which his head is broken and he suffers great pain. Now you see that the house was not built by God, it was built by artisans and that the brick or stone or wood etc was not placed there by God, and God did not throw it or break his head. That brick or stone or wood was worn out by time. The brick etc being either worn out by time or moved by any man or animal or wind broke his head and caused him pain. But this was not caused by God. Consequently God has not created various kinds of pleasure and pain, highness and lowness in this world. On the other hand, by *prawah* (unbroken succession) this variegated universe comes into being and to end caused by the *nimits* such as the mutual action of time, *swabhao* (nature), *niyati* (rules of conduct), *karma* (action), *purushârth* (any one of the four principal objects of human life i. e. *dharma*, *arth*, *kam*, *moksha*), matter ; and it would remain so from eternity to eternity. The *moksa-pad* is also without beginning and end. The living beings do attain that position having destroyed all the actions. The worldly beings come into human or other life and enjoy pleasure or suffer pain and get high or low position etc. with the help of their respective causes *nimits* according to their good or bad actions. Arhat-Siddha Parmeshar-knows from his knowledge all the different conditions of the worldly beings who are doing good or bad actions and suffering their consequences with the help of *nimits*. Everything is done just in the same way as God reflects in his knowledge. Nothing is done contrary to it.

88 Q.—What short-comings are there in all the religions ?

A.—Nobody calls the religion believed in by him to be faulty. People are always ready to point out faults in other religions. The Jaina religion is entirely faultless. But in the present age the Indian Jainas do not possess such mental and physical energies as may enable them to completely tread the path of *moksha* as dictated by the Jaina shâstras. The Jainas pass the lives of a recluse and householder according to the present age. But they cannot completely follow the *Utsargik* (natural, that which is liable to be abolished in exceptional cases, though generally valid) path. The second defect among the Jainas is that they pay little heed towards education. There is no union among them. Even the *Sâdhus* are not on good terms among themselves. These defects are in the individual Jainas of the present age, while the Jaina religion is faultless.

89 Q.—What have Judaism, Christianity and other religions done for mankind ?

A.—These religions have done *limited* good to

mankind by preaching through their religious books to mankind the worship of God, mercy, charity, truth, chastity, contentment, forgiveness, *ârjava* (honesty), *mârdava* (gentleness), *vinaya* (respect, politeness), obligingness, *kratajnatâ* (grate fulness) etc., which give a good name to such persons in this world and *swarg* (heaven,) kingdom etc. But the religions referred to above, have done great harm to mankind in as much as they have not told mankind the true attributes of *Deva* (God) *guru* (teacher) and *dharma* and have teachings to the contrary. The Jaina religion shows for mankind *ekant hit* (wholesome good) and the true path of *moksha* and nothing perverted. Hence it has done all good without harm.

90 Q.—How did the people come to understand the importance of the formula of repentance?

A.—First the repentance does away with the sin which has been done unknowingly. This is not the case with all sorts of sins.

Some sinful acts become relax by repentance. The good of repentance lies only in this that he who repents for a sinful act does not do that act again. The reason why the conviction in the formula of repentance is essential is that the person who fears the consequences of sinful act, repents purely from his heart, then his heart becomes very soft, and the very pervasiveness of that purity and softness in the heart destroys all sins. The formula of repentance has been dictated by the omniscient God who is free from 18 faults. God never speaks falsehood. Thus formerly in the time of *sarvajna Parmeshwar*, Gautama and other *munis* (saints) believed in the truth of the formula. In other words, their speeches made the people believe in it. This is the *siddhânt* (doctrine).

91. Q.—Is it necessary to have a fixed day to take rest for doing *dharma* ?

A.—One should always remain engaged in doing *dharma*, of course one who does not get time to do *dharma* may fix particular days for doing *dharma*. For such a person it is necessary to have fixed days for doing *dharma*. One who is independent (or self controlled) must always do *dharma*. It is essential to fix a day for giving up sinful acts. No day is meant for pleasure, enjoyment, play etc.

92 Q.—Who is believed to be an *avatâr* by religionists ?

A.—With the exception of Jainism many other religions do believe that God being *mukti rup*-liberated from the shuffles of actions and bodiless,-can come in the world as an *avatâr*. The cause of coming as an *avatâr* arises when there is a fall in virtue and the *sâdhus* and other good men are in trouble. In order to remove these evils and to do good to others and to destroy evil souls, the enemies of *dharma*, God takes an *avatâr* in every age. Such is the statement in Gita. The Buddhists say that when the propagator of their religion viz. *bhagwân* having attained the highest stage of *moksha* sees his followers in trouble, in order to remove their troubles, he takes an *avatar*. The Christians believe that for the good of the sinful descendants of man, God sent his Son Christ on the earth.

The Jains believe that after attaining liberation nobody comes back in this world, in as much as the causes of possessing body are good and bad *karmas*. On the attainment of *moksha* all karmas are destroyed. For this reason the Jainas do not believe that a soul after attainment of *moksha* takes an *avatâr*.

It has been described above how the Jainas believe in *arhats*.

The followers of Vedas, Smritis, and Purans believe Bramha, Vishnu and Maheshwar to be the *avatârs* of God. Some of them believe in 24 *avatârs* of God such as *machh*, *sukar*, *kachhu*, *narsingh* etc. The others believe Patanjali, Shankar Swami, Ramanuja and others to be the *avatârs* of God. Wherever there is any renowned man, his followers in their books speak of him as the *avatâr* of God. In India always after some time a new religion antagonistic to the other, comes into being through a person—so called *avatâr* of God. It is not known why God is so kind to Indians in as much as He comes here so often as an *avatâr*. But the allegation that after attainment of *moksha* God comes in this world as avatar, is against reason and logic because all the different religions believe God to be omnipotent. When God is omnipotent, can He not do every thing He likes without occupying a body. If He could do every thing without occupying a body, what was the necessity for him to come in the womb of a woman. Why did He not make proper arrangement in the beginning so that there would not have been any mismanagement and He would not have stood in need of coming here as *avatär* to put things into proper order.

Many religionists believe that God is all-pervading. But he who is all-pervading is *akria* (motionless) i.e. one who can not do anything regarding motion like *âkâsh* (sky). If God is all-pervading, all powerful, merciful, well-wisher of all living beings and preacher of the true religion, where-in the religious Samajic disputes arise which create ill-feellings in worldly and religious matters among the people and cause the death of lacs of people and become the cause of many other troubles and calamities etc. why does not then God who is in those *sakahas* and who is merciful, all-pervading and all-powerful say at once that this is true and this is false and that one particular thing be done and the other avoided and that such is his statement which shows the true path and the others not. When in order to remove the troubles of the worldly beings God by remaining in the womb of woman and then having been born saves them from their enemies, why can he not remove those troubles at once without adopting the above procedure. If he cannot adopt the latter procedure, He cannot be proved to be omnipotent.

What is the cause of it that God comes as an *avatâr* in one country and not in the other. Bramha, Vishnu and Mahesh came as avatârs in India only. The Christ was born in the eastern country and not in any other country. God sent Mohamad also in Arab only. Can God not take the form of Brahma, Vishnu, Mahâdeva, Christ, Mohamad etc. as *avatârs* in all the different countries and send also all foolish and barbarous people to Moksha by preaching them.

93 Q.—The 24 Tirthankaras among the Jainas were also born in Aryavarta. Hence the aforesaid defect is also present there ?

A.—My dear sir, had the Tirthankaras adopted this position of their own will, the aforesaid defect would have been said to be found in them. The Jains do not believe in it. Hence that defect cannot be imputed to them.

94 Q.—According to Jainas what is the cause for becoming a Tirthankara ?

A.—A living being who has done very good *karma* is born as a Tirthankara by reason of those good *karmas* and not of his own accord.

95 Q.—As the Tirthankar also is bound by the *karmas*, He can do nothing without *karmas*. Hence why should he be believed to be God ?

A.—No one in the world (except Jainas) believes in such God as *arhat* who has been free from 18 defects and who possessed such qualities as infinite knowledge etc. real happiness etc. Consequently the *arhat* himself is Parmeshwar and none else. The people in general believe in God to be the Lord of the universe like sovereigns. But according to their own allegations no God as believed in by them has been proved to be free from 18 faults. On the other hand, according to their *Shastras*, God is partial, cruel, ignorant, passionate, proud, ill-tempered, unjust, wicked, incompetent and powerless.

96 Q.—How can we believe that Arhat Parmeshwar

was free from 18 defects and that the *avatâr* of God believed in by others had those faults ?

A.—My dear Sir, leaving aside prejudice, read the lives of Arhats and other *avatârs* etc. and see their images noticing their conduct, thoughts and appearance ; from this you would learn which of them was faulty and which faultless.

97 Q.—The Jainas have written well about their Tirthankaras and have also made their images *shânt* (contented), *dânt* (mild) *nirvikâri* (without change of mind or purpose), aloof from woman, of desire-less forms.

A.—This idea of yours is wrong in as much as none prevented the writers of your sacred books from writing the good qualifications of your *avatârs* and none told them to write the bad qualifications of your *avatârs* such as a certain *avatâr* had intercourse with another's wife, another *avatâr* wandered with one's (sister), another *avatâr* wandered in the jungle on account of his separation from his wife, another *avatâr* being naked danced before a Rishi who gave him a curse whereupon his male organ was broken into pieces, another *avatâr* caused a battle to be fought and was himself engaged in it, another *avatâr* caused falsehood to be spoken, another *avatâr* was tired of going, another *avatâr* went to eat *gular* fruits and not finding the fruits on the trees gave it a curse to be dried up and it was dried up, another *avatâr* infused life in a dead body, at the time of his death had himself hanged, wished to remain alive but could not, died when the time of the death arrived, could not remain alive till now, that God created people of a certain community when those people did not act up to His dictates, He repented and having become angry destroyed certain cities and gave so many Curses etc. Many such statements are found in their books. Had not those *avatârs* possessed those qualifications, the writers would have not made a mention of those improper things. The writers were not their enemies on account of which enmity they might have written improper things. If they wrote falsely their books are not to be accepted. Thus it has been fully proved that the *avatârs* of the people were of such character as mentioned in their books. Bharatrahari praises Cupid for having made slaves of the highest gods when they are attacked by the amorous dances of pretty and charming women.

Consequently the writers of the times of the 24 Tirthankaras wrote their lives just as they actually were. Thus the biographies and the images of the avatârs fully prove their faults and faultlessness.

98 Q.—What are the biographies and qualities of the Tirthankaras ?

If you want to read the biographies of the twenty four Jaina Tirthankaras in the historical form, please read the Trishash-tishalâkâ-purush-charitra by Hemachandra Sûri. I give you a brief account of the life of the blessed Lord Mahâvira, the last Tirthankara.

In the *Videhdesh* (ancient Mithila country) in Ksatriya-Kunda-grâma, there was a Raja named Siddhârtha, in the Sûrya-Vansha or Jnâtavansha.

He had a queen Trishlâ, who gave birth to a child on Tuesday, Chaitra Sudi 13th at night in the 1st part of Uttrâ Phâlguni Nakchhatra, 542 years before Vikram Samvat. (i.e. about 600 B.C.) The parents gave him the birth name of Vardhmâna. When he attained maturity his parents married him with Yashodhâ, the daughter of Sidhârtha's feudatory Samarvir. When he became 28 years of age, his parents died. After that he remained in the family for 2 years at the request of his elder brother i.e. he remained in the house till he was aged 30 years and had one daughter named Priayadarshanâ. After that he took initiation in the sâdhu life, with the permission of his elder brother Nandivardhan. For one year he kept a piece of cloth placed on his shoulder by Indra ? Subsequently he went about without clothes for the whole life. Although troubles befell him, he did not swerve from his true vow. Thereupon the *devtâs* (good spirits) named him Mahâvira. After his initiation, he renounced to commit or make others commit injury to living beings, he gave up speaking falsehood, theft, sexual intercourse, etc. He not only gave up all these sins himself but also prohibited others from doing them. He possessed threefold knowledge from his birth. Just at the time of initiation he obtained the 4th knowledge viz. *manparyây*. The blessed Mahâvira Lord practised great austerities for 12½ years. It is fully described in Avashyak Sûtra and Kalpa sûtra etc. what different troubles befell him for 12½ years and at what different places and how he calmly and quietly bore all of them. What by means of the practice of austerities for 12½ years and full meditation of virtue he completely destroyed his four *ghati karmas* (those which obstruct the good qualities of soul), then in the last *pahâr* (a period of three hours) on Vaisâkh Sudi 10th he attained *Keval jnâna* (perfect knowledge) onthe bank of the Rijuvâlukâ river in the village of Jram-bhika. He having left the aforesaid place arrived at Madhya-Pâpâ Nagri. At that place there were eleven well-known Brahmans headed by Indrabhuti,-Gautam,-all learned in fourteen sciences. He removed all the doubts entertained by them in accordance with the Veda Srutis and by logical reasons and made the above mentioned eleven personages and their 4400 students as his desciples by performing their *diksha* ceremony. Out of them those (eleven) i. e. Gautam and others were given the title of Gandhara. They compiled the teachings of the Bhagvant in the books such as Achârânga etc. He also gave *diksha* to Chandnâ the virgin daughter of king Dadhivâhan of Champâ who made 36000 desciples.

After the attainment of pure knowledge (*Keval jnâna*) he visited countries on the eastern side. In the life time of Lord Mahavira there were not more than 14000 *sadhus*, 46000 *sadhwis*, 159,000 *srâvaks* and 3,18000 *srâvikâs*. The lectures of

Lord Mahavira made several chiefs His votaries. They are as follows :—

(I) Raja Srenika *alias* Bhambhasâra, King of Rajagrihi.

(II) Ashoka Chandra *alias* Kunik king of Champâ, son of Bhambha sâra. In the Buddhistic books he is named as Ajâtshatru.

(III) Raja Chetaka, king of Vaishâli nagrî.

(XXI) A group of 18 Rajas of Kashi and Kaushal.

(XXII) Vijaya king of Pulâspur.

(XXIII) Sveta king of Amalkalpâ Nagri.

(XXIV) Raja Udâyan of Vitbhai-patan in sindh.

(XXV) Raja Udayanvatsa of Kaushambhi.

(XXVI) Raja Nandi-Vardhan of Ksatriya kundagram.

(XXVII) Raja Chandra Pradyota of Ujjain.

(XXVIII) Raja Shâl of Prishta Champa.

(XXIX) Raja Prasanna Chandra of Potanpur.

(XXX) Raja Adin Shatru of Hasti Shirsha nagar.

(XXXI) Raja Dhanavah of Rishabhpur.

(XXXII) Raja Vir Krishnamitra of Virpur nagar.

(XXXIII) Raja Vasavdatta of Vijaipur.

(XXXIV) Raja Pratihat of Saugandhik.

(XXXV) Priya Chandra, king of Kanakpur.

(XXXVI) Raja Bal of Mahapur.

(XXXVII) Raja Arjun of Sughosh nagar.

(XXXVIII) Râjâ Datta of Champâ.

(XXXIX) Râjâ Mitra Nandi of Saketpur.

(XL) Raja Dashârn Bhadra of Dasharnpur, and many other Rajas were the followers of Lord Mahâvîra. The names of all these are found in the works known as Angas and Upangas. He lived 42 years after his initiation *dikshâ*. Out of this period he passed first 12 Chaturmâsas (period of 4 months of the rainy season i.e. Shavan, Bhadrapad Ashwin and Kartiq) as *chhadamast* (passing saint's life before *kevalagnâna*) and the subsequent 30 Chaturmâsas as Kevalî as given below :—

The first 12 rainy seasons 1. Asthigrâma, 2. Râjagrihi, 3. Champâ. 4. Prishta Champâ, 5. Bhadrikâ nagri, 6. Bhadrika, 7. Alambhiyâ, 8. Râjgrihi, 9. Anâryadesh, 10. Sâvathî, 11. Vishâlâ, 12. Champâ.

As *Kevali* He passed 12 rainy seasons in Râjgrihi, 11 in Vishala, 6 in Mithila and 1 in Pâvâpuri. Out of 42 years, for 30 years Lord Mahavira taught *dharma* to all the 4 classes and spread dharma. He had his last rainy season at Pâvâpuri in the sabhâ of the old office of the king Hstipâlâ. He attained nirvana i.e. *Muktipad*, *Siddhapad*, *Parmeshwâr-pâd* (liberation) on Kartik vadi 15th at night.

According to the test just described the *avatârs* believed in by other religionists, were not free from 18 faults. It was only Arhat who was free from 18 *dushans* (faults). The God believed in by other religionists is according to their own allegations proved to be ignorant, incompetent, having liking and disliking, merciless, prejudiced, imprudent etc. Consequently there is no God besides *Arhat* and *Siddha.* This is the main doctrine of Jainas.

The Siddha does not concern himself with the affairs of the world. The blessed Arhat teaches only Dharma. He does not do any worldly work except teaching dharma. This proves that Arhat and Siddha Bhagvân are free from 18 *dushans* (faults).

It is an impossible task to describe the qualities of God, yet I attempt to write something about the qualities of *Arhat pad.* Arhat Bhagvân being desireless of any gain in exchange, gives right instructions which are holy and noble and are like rafts to take across the ocean of the mundane existence, to the king and the poor, the Brahman and the chandâl i.e. all classes of persons alike. He possesses 1. infinite knowledge 2. infinite vision 3. infinite character 4. infinite austerity, 5. infinite power, 6. infinite fine gifts, 7. forgiveness, 8. greedlessness, 9. simplicity. 10. pridelessness, 11. humility, 12. truth, 13. self control, 14. desirelessness, 15. chastity, 16. mercy, 17. doing good to others, 18. absence of attachment, 19. absence of disliking, 20. fearlessness, 21. absence of hatred, 22. absence of laughter, 23. absence of shock, 24. absence of pleasure, 25. absence of pain. 26. passionlessness, 27. absence of superstition, 28 absence of ignorance, 29. sleeplessness, 30. absence of indifference 31. absence of idea of friendship and enmity, 32. equal regard for gold and stone, 33. equal regard for woman and grass, 34. avoidance of flesh diet, 35. avoidance of intoxicating drugs, 36. avoidance of eating uneatables, 37. fathomless mercy, 38. bravery, 39. strength, 40. fortitude, 41. serenity, 42. absence of speaking ill of others, 43. absence of self-praise, 44. power to cause, through preachings, the salvation of those who have ill feelings towards him and who disgrace him and speak ill of him, etc. etc.

The qualities of Arhat and Siddha both together are 1. *Avyaya* (immortal) 2. glorious 3. Achintya (beyond thought), 4. incalculable, 5. Primeval, 6. Brahma, (possessor of infinite happiness) 7. Ishwar (Lord of devas), 8. Anant (Infinite) 9. The destroyer of cupid, 10, Lord of Yogis, 11. proficient in Yoga, 12. manifold, 13. One, 14, pure intelligence, 15. immaculate.

Each of these attributes is explained as follows :—

1. Immortal is that which exists in all times-past, present and future. (2) Glorious because he shines as the Lord over all gods such as Indra and others. (3) Beyond thought because even mental contemplation is unable to grasp him. (4) Incalculable because his qualities can not be calculated as they are beyond all enumeration. 5. Primeval or first because he leads the path to righteousness in the world. 6. Brahma because he is the seat of infinite happiness. 7. Ishwar because

he is the Lord of all Gods. 8. Infinite because he is endowed with infinite knowledge and wisdom or because he has no end. 9. Destroyer of Cupid because he destroys Cupid as the rising sun dispels darkness or (one who has not faculties liable to the influences of Cupid.) one who has not got any sort of body. 10. Yogishwer because he is the Lord of the Yogis possessing fourfold knowledge. 11. Proficient in Yoga because he has grasped all the secrets of Yoga, or he has broken asunder all association with the *karma*. 12. Manifold because he is omniscient and omnipresent through knowledge. 13. One because he is secondlessly best. 14. Pure intelligence because he lives and moves and have his being in pure knowledge. 15. Immaculate because he is free from 18 faults.

These fifteen attributes are given to God by religionists who believe in Him.

The following are some of the innumerable attributes of a Siddha.

He is beyond 1. destruction, 2. oldage, 3. death, 4. change or motion, 5. consumption, 6. impurity, 7. mutibilily, 8. form ; He is the 9. form of refulgence, 10. the Lord, 11. the supreme being, 12. the highest spirit, 13. the form of existence intelligence and bliss, 14. the unborn, 15. the one not to be born again.

99. Q.—What are the mutual relations of faiths or Dharma ?

A.—Dharma is related to the soul as subject and attribute and truth is the connecting link of all the religions in the world and it is truth which is loved.

100 Q.—In what way is the Dharma connected with physical science, arts and literature ?

A.—Dharma is related to the physical science as knowledge and knowable, to arts which are not above suspicions, as some thing to be avoided and to arts which are innocent, as acceptable, to literature which promotes spiritual knowledge and vision.

101 Q.—In what way can religious books, natural science, political economy and sociology help the Dharma shâstra ?

A.—By religious books I mean the sacred books of every religion. The truth in every sacred book is helpful to the progress of righteousness and the untruth therein is a sort of set back to it. The books on physical science disclose many of the infinite forces which are mentioned in the religious books to be working by combination of matter and force. Consequently the books on physical science help in supporting the truth contained in the sacred love. By Jivan shâstra, I mean political economy. If money is earned by honest means, *jivan* shâstra is helpful in furthering the object of *dharma shâstra.* If money is earned by dishonest means, it would cause sin and it goes against *dharma shâstra.* The Vaidik shâstra is helpful in spreading dharma shâstra by removing diseases. By *samajik* shâstra I mean *niti shâstra* As *niti shâstra* makes man do work lawfully in the world it promotes the injunctions of the *dharma shâstra.* Consequently *niti shâstra* is also helpful to the *dharma shâstra.*

102 Q.—In what manner can religious books help the other scientific books ? What is the connection between dharma and music ?

A.—The *dharma shâstra* helps the shâstras of other sciences only to a small extent and not entirely. The *dharma* shâstra is helpful to all that is written in the shâstra of other sciences according as it supports or is antagonistic to them. The praise of Parmeshwar, teacher and dharma or the attributes of dharma and the virtues of a dharmic person in verse, song or music causes the belief of a hearer to be firm in dharma and stores good *karmas* for him and causes the destruction of *karmas* and *punya bandha* to the singer. One who sings a song exciting delusion or lust would have the bondage of sin and would be degenerated in the next life.

103 Q.—How far is *dharma* effective in perfectly purifying human being ?

A.—Dharma has a very great effect in this respect in as much as it is *dharma* which can make a human being attain *Ishvar-pad.* No stage is higher or purer than this.

104 Q.—How can one who has gone astray from the dharma be purified ?

A.—The blessed Arhat, who is free from 18 defacts, in order to purify the fallen persons has explained theshastras, as, Sraddha jît-Kalpa, Yatijit-kapla, Nishith, Kalpa, Vayavhâra. The aforesaid books describe 10 kinds of *prâyashchitta* (penances) for purifying fallen persons. The nature of purification takes with the nature of transgression in each particular case. The purificartory rites prescribed for a householder are different from those for the sâdhus. One who takes the prescribed penance and then acts upon it, becomes purified like a clothing from which a blot is removed.

105. Q.—Many people make sacrifices to Parmeshvar in order to attain liberation *moksha*. Is it essential or not ?

A.—Those who make sacrifices to Parmeshvara by killing living beings, are greatly mistaken because Parmeshvara is without passion, most merciful, always desireless. No work whatever pleases or displeases him. Thus to kill living beings and make sacrifices for him is a great sin. This practice has been brought into existence by most ignorant persons. This would appear from the Jainamata-vriksa compiled by me.

106. Q.—What bearing has *dharma* on the progress of the country ?

A.—The country is a progressive one in which on account of the spread of dharma such good actions are done as to follow the rules of law, to have union among themselves, to do good to others, to be kind to all living beings, to speak truth, not to cheat or defraud, to acquire knowledge always, to lead a contented life, to avoid committing theft, adultery, taking *abhaksha*, drinking prohibited things, practising superstitious rites. The progress of a country is impossible without dharma.

107. Q.—How should the king and the customs be followed ?

A.—If the King gives legal orders they ought to be followed and the useful customs put in vogue by good persons must certainly be followed. The customs the non-observance of which is liable to cause material and spiritual loss to us by the country city or community, ought to be followed.

108. Q.—What are the perfect attributes of dharma found among the different religions ? What are the eventual objects of dharma.

A.—The perfect attributes of dharma are three in number viz. (1) *Darshana* (belief), (2) *jnâna* (knowledge), (3) *chûritra* (action) Darshana means belief in *tatvas*. The *Tatvas* are three viz. *deva*, *guru*, *dharma*. By the term *deva* is meant master. Master is one who is free from 18 *dushans* (defects), is possessed of 12 *gunas* (virtues), and is the preacher of true dharma in this world and is after giving up this body to become the Siddha. There is no God other than such God. To worship such a benevolent master for the purpose of purifying one's own soul, to publish His qualities in the world according to his ability to praise Him always are acts helpful to one's spiritual development. This is called *Shudha devatatva*. Guru (teacher) is one who observes 5 *maha-vratas* (highest vows), who is well-versed in sacred lore, has always uniformity of disposition, gets pure food i.e. free from any fault by means of begging, maintains thereby his body for the purpose of doing good, possesses many other such qualities and tells the people in the world what has been preached by the aforesaid masters. This is *Gurutatva.* The aforesaid masters have shown to the people the path (Law) which leads to salvation. This is *dharma tatva* What is contrary to those three is called (1) Kudeva (false Master, (2) ku-guru (false teacher) (3) Ku-dharma (false law.) One ought to believe in the truth of master, teacher, and law and wholly abandon *kudeva, Ku-guru, ku-dharma-* Thus one attains the first part (attribute) of dharma named *Darshan.* There are five divisions of Jnana (knowledge) *i.e.*, (1) mati-Jnana (knowledge through senses, (2) *Sruti-jnana* (knowledge by means of education) (3) *avadhi-jnana* (knowledge of *forming* matter to a certain extent) (4) *man-pray-ay jnana* (knowledge of the mental thought of living beings born of pregnancy in 2½ *dvipas*, (5) *Keval jnana* (perfect knowledge). The objects of these 5 kinds of knowledge are six dravyas and nine tattvas. This is 2nd part of dharma named *jnana.* The third part of dharma is *châritra.* It is divided into 140 parts by reason of the divisions of *charana sattari and karanâ-sattari.* The divisions of *charana sattari are* (1) five *Mahavratas* (2) *ten Yati dharma* (3) seventeen *sanyam* (self-control) (4) ten *vaiyâ-vrityas* (services) (5) nine *brahmacharya gupti*, (6) three jnâna, darshan and châritra, (7) twelve tapas (8) control of *krodh* (anger) etc. These are 70 in number. The 70 divisions of *karana sattari* are :—

(1) 4 kinds of bodily purification.
(2) 5 kinds of *sammiti*
(3) 12 kinds of meditations
(4) 12 kinds of *pratimâs*
(5) 5 kinds of control of senses
(6) 25 Pratilekhna
(7) 3 Guptis
(8) 4 kinds of Abhigrhaha

Thus there are 140 divisions of *charitra* in all. This is third part of dharma.

An Explanatory list of words, phrases sentences &c. in the book.

93 Actions that interfere with the performance or enjoyment of good things [*Antarâya Karma*]

98 Actions that impede Soul's progress [*Ghati Karmâs*]. The four karmas viz. Gnanâvarniya, Darsnâvarniya, Mohniya, and Antarâya are called Ghati Karmâs.

40 Advaitism. Vedantic doctrine propounded by Shri Shanker-Acharya.

148 Afflictions [*Parisahâs*] These are 22. For further details, see Uttaradyayana, 2nd chapter.

155 Agnibhuti. 1st Ganadhar of Lord Mahavir.

155 Akampita. 8th Ganadhar of Lord Mahavir.

92 Anger. [*Krodha*]. There are 18 *Papasthâns* : this is 6th.

153 Another purpose [*Apavâda*]. Special rule.

87 Apparent forms [*Paryâya*].

132 *Apân.* One kind of winds moving in a body.

110 *Arhat.* One free from 18 *doshas*—18 faults. These 18 faults are enumerated at p. 110-13. He is also called Arihant, one who has destroyed inner enemies i.e. *Raga*—passion, and *Dvesha*—hatred.

154 Aristnemi. 22nd Tirthanker of the Jains.

98 *Avadhi.* Knowledge independent of senses, comprising limited objects.

123 Atom. [*Parmânu*]

150 Baldev—Elder brother of Vasudeva, who is the king of 3 continents.

99 *Bahushruta*—One learned in many shastras.

190 Belief in Tatvas –[*Darshan*].

121 Bhutâs—Five material elements—Earth, Water, Fire, Wind and Sky.

16 Brahma—One of the Puranic Gods believed to be the creator of the world by the Hindus.

16 Buddhists—Followers of Lord Buddha.

92 Calumny. [*Abhyâkhyân*]. 13th Papasthân.

40 Canon of Real existence of phenomena [*Satakhyâti*].

176 Chandnâ. Virgin daughter of king Dadhivâhan. She was the first among Shrâvikâs to be initiated in Jain Diksha by Lord Mahavir. She is known as Chandnabâlâ.

150 Chakravarti. King of 6 continents : Bharat was the 1st Chakravarti in the beginning of this cycle.

120 Chârvâkâs—Followers of an ancient school of Indian philosophy, who do not believe in soul.

143 *Chaityavanda*-Bow to idols repeating God's virtues.

127 Characteristics [*Linga*] (Reasons).

145 Characteristics of Dharma. These are ten and are given at p. 145.

192 *Charansattari.*

178 *Chhadmasta.* Passing saint's life before Kevalgnana.

152 *Chhed shudha shastra.*

87 Continuity. [*Niyati*] (Futurity). Also translated as Law of Continuity. There are five causes in production of any effect. This is 3rd.

136 Concomitant cause [*Sahakari Karan*].

121 Consciousness [*Svasamvedana*].

57 Contradictory [*Virudha Hetvabhasa*].

92 Covetousness [*Lobha*] 9th Papasthan.

109 Delusion [*Mithyâtva*].

92 Desire [*Vasnâ*].

190 *Deva Tatva.*

190 *Dharma Tatva.*

98 *Dharma Tirtha*—Teaching of twelve Angâs, the sacred books ; as well as the establishment of the fourfold Sangha.

112 Disgust—[*Jugupsâ*].

146 Duty of a householder [*Grihasta Dharma*].

140 Eight-fold devotion. [*Asta Prakâri Pujâ*]. Its description begins from p. 141.

84 Energy [*Udyama*] 5th Cause in an effect, also translated as 'motive power'.

19 Eternal truths [*Arya Satyas*]. Buddha's doctrine. These are four viz. *Dukkha*, *Samuchya*, *Mârga*, and *Nirodha*.

92 Extortion. [*Parigrah*] 8th Papasthân.

92 False utterances [*Mâyâmrishâvâda*] 17th Papasthân.

92 Falsehood [*Mrishâvâda*] 2nd Papasthân.

26 Fallacy of mutual dependence [*Itaratarâsâyadosha*].

40 Fallacy of perverse knowledge [*Viprita khyâti*].

24 Fallacy of reasoning in a circle [*Anavasthâ dosha*].

92 Future action (*Prârabdha Karma.*)

143 Going on pilgrimage. [*Tirtha yâtra*].

150 Great vows [*Mahâvratas*]. These are five and observed by Sadhus.

190 *Gurutatva.*

92 Hatred [*Dvesha*] 11th Papasthân.

92 Illusion [*Mâyâ*] (Deceipt). 8th Papasthân.

101 Infinite pure knowledge [*Anant keval gnana*].

„ Infinite pure vision [*Anant keval Darsan*].

„ Infinite fivefold possessions [*Anant Pancha Labdhis*].

„ Infinite power of action [*Anant Charitra*].

155 Indrabhuti—1st Ganadhar of Mahavir.

92 Injury to living beings [*Jivahinsa*] 1st Papasthan.

150 Inner enemies [*Antara Vairies*]. These are six.

185 Innocent [*Nirvadya*].

18 Jaimini's Doctrine—Doctrine propounded by the Sage Jaimini. It is known as the Purva Mimansa Darsan.

92 Jealousy [*Paishunaya*] 14th Papasthân

152 *Kash Shudha Shastra.*

192 *Karan sittari.*

92 Like or dislike sentiments [*Rati, arati*] 15th Papasthân.

98 Liberation [*Moksha*]. Jains believe in nine Tatvas. This is the 9th Tatva.

98 *Lokântika*—Celestial beings, whose duty is to come to the would-be Tirthanker and say 'Oh Bhagwan, show the path of virtue and rectitude'.

16 *Madhukari Bhikshâ.* Particular kind of begging : just as a bee tastes the flowers without passion, so do the Sâdhus beg.

155 Mahavir Swami. 24th Tirthanker of the Jains.

175 *Manaparyây.* Knowledge of the thoughts of those living in $2\frac{1}{2}$ dvipâs.

155 Manditputra. 6th Ganadhar of Lord Mahavir.

57 Many-sided. [*Anekântic dosha*].

47 Material cause [*Upâdânkâran*].

98 *Mati*—Knowledge obtained by means of five senses and mind.

155 Metârya—10th Ganadhar of Lord Mahavir.

16 Mimânsakâs—Followers of the Mimânsâ school of philosophy, known as Jaiminiya Darsan. This school is known as Purva Mimânsâ.

99 *Mulgunâs*—Five great vows—non killing, truth, non-stealing, chastity and extortion observed by the sâdhus.

155 Muaryaputra. 7th Ganadhar of Lord Mahavir.

17 Nature [*Svabhâva*]. One of the causes in the production of the effect.

92 Nature [*Prakrati*]. Special term used by the Sânkyâs for matter, as opposed to soul.

16 Naiyâyikâs—Followers of an ancient school of Hindu philosophy propounded by the sage Akshapâd. (Gautama).

110 Obstruction to unstinted distribution of charity [*Danântarâyâ*].

" Obstruction to unstinted possession [*Labhântarâya*].

" Obstruction to unstinted powers [*Viryântarâya*].

111 Obstruction to unstinted new enjoyments, such as flowers, garlands etc [*Bhogântarâya*].

111 Obstruction to unstinted daily enjoyments such as woman, apparells etc [*Upbhogântaráya*].

152 One purpose [*Utsarga*]. general rule.

147 *Panch-Parmesti*—A collective name for the five adepts viz—the Arhat, the Siddha, the Acharyas, the Upadyayas, the Sadhus.

104 Patanjalists—Followers of Yoga Darsan—an ancient Hindu School of philosophy propounded by the sage Patanjli.

92 Passion. [*Râga*] 10th Papasthân.

92 Past action [*Sanchita*].

187 Penances [*Prayachhita*].

175 Period of three hours [*Pahar*].

147 *Poshad Vrata*.

155 Prabhâs. 11th Ganadhar of Lord Mahavir.

155 Prabhâswâmi. Pupil of Jambuswâmi—last Kewali.

100 *Pravchana*—Name generally used for the Jain Agamas.

92 Present action (*Kriyamân*).

174 Priyadarsnâ—Daughter of Mahavir.

92 Pride [*Mân*] 7th Papasthana.

132 *Prân*—Breath.

60 Quality of pervasion (*Vyâpti*). Invariable association of Sâdya and Linga.

92 Quarrel [*Kalah*] 12th Papasthan.

166 Ramânuj—He is a propounder of the Vishistâdvait school of philosophy. His chief work is a commentary on Vedant Sutras.

143 *Rathyâtra*. Taking the image of God in a chariot along with a procession.

100 Reverence to Scriptures. [*Sruta Bhakti*].

99 Right-seeing [*Darsan*, *Samyaktwa*].

18 Sânkya doctrine—Teaching of sage Kapila. It forms one of the ancient schools of Hindu philosophy. The followers of this doctrine are called Sânkyâs.

92 Scandal. [*Paraparivâda*] 15th Papasthân.

98 Self-enlightened [*Kevali*] one who destroys four kinds of Ghati karmas and obtains infinite knowledge etc.

99 Self-control [*Samvega*].

92 Sentimental grievance [*Mithyatwa Salya*] 18th Papasthân.

92 Sexual intercourse [*Maithun*] 4th Papasthân.

16 Shiva. One of the Puranic Gods believed by the Hindus. The followers of this God are called Shaivites.

47 Shanker-Acharya—He is a propounder of the Advait Vedant. His chief work is a commentary on Vedant Sutras.

174 Siddhârtha—Father of Lord Mahavir.

18 *Siddhi.*

126 Size [*Samsthâna*].

98 *Sruta*—Knowledge obtained from the Agamâs, through their interpretation.

155 Svayambhav. Author of Dasvaikâlik-sutra and the pupil of Prabhavsvâmi.

92 Subtle body of desire [*Kârman Sarira*]. Body made of karmas : it accompanies the soul from all eternity.

155 Sudharma. 5th Ganadhara of Lord Mahavir.

153 *Tapshudhi Shastra.*

19 Teaching [*Tirtha*].

92 Theft [*Adattâdan*] 3rd Papasthân.

17 Time. [*Kâl*] one of the five causes of effect.

18 Tirthanker.

174 Trislâ—Mother of Lord Mahavir.

98 Twenty-virtues [*Visha- sthânkas*]. The description of these begins from p. 99.

148 Troubles (*Parisahâs*). They are 16 in number, for further details see Uttaradhyayan 2nd chapter.

47 Upnishads—Original works forming the last part of the Vedas and treating of Atma and Paramatma.

162 *Utsargic.*

99 *Uttargunâs*—Purification of food etc. These are observed by the Sadhus. These are in connection with Mulgunas.

Uttarmimânsâ—doctrine propounded by sage Vyasa. It forms one of the ancient Schools of Hindu philosophy. The followers of this school are called Vedantis.

19 Vaisesik doctrine—doctrine propounded by Sage Kanâda. It is called by 'Vaisesik' because the sage believed 'Visesa' as one of the Categories. This also forms an ancient Hindu School of philosophy.

Brief notes on the works alluded to in the book.

Page.

176 Achârânga. 1st Anga sutra ; Shri Bhadrabâhuswâmi has composed a Niryukti upon it. The Niryukti with the Sutra is commented by Shri Shilângachârya. Translated in the Sacred Books of the East Series Vol. XXII. Published with the commentary by Agamodayasmiti, Surat.

95 Anekântjaypatâkâ. The author is Shri Hari-bhadrasuri : the same is the commentator. It deals with Syadvâd. Published by seth Mansukhbhai Bhagubhai, Ahmedabad.

96 Aptamimânsa. The author is Shri Samantbhadra-acharya : commentator is Shri Vidyanandsuri : commentary is known as Astasahsri (To be had at Hindi Grantha Ratnaker Karyalaya, Bombay). The commentary is further commented by Shri Yashovijayji.

100 Avasyakasutra. 1st Mula Sutra, dealing with higher principles of Jain philo-

sophy, and history. Shri Bhadrabâhuswâmi has composed a Niryukti upon it. The Niryukti has been commented by Shri Haribhadrasuri. Published by Agamodayasamiti, Surat. There are also another commentaries on it by many Acharyas.

119 Bhagavati—5th Anga Sutra, commented by Shri Abhaydevasuri. It deals with 36000 questions and answers between Gotama and Mahavir. Published in Babu Dhanpatsinghji Series, Calcutta.

154 Dasvaikalika Sutra. 2nd Mula Sutra. Composed by Shri Svayambhavswâmi and commented by Shri Haribhadrasuri. It deals with rules of conduct for ascetics. Published by Bhimsi Manek Bombay.

96 Dharmasanghrani. The author is Shri Haribhadrasuri. The work is in Prakrit verses. The commentator is Shri Malaygiriji. It deals with all systems of philosophy. Published by Devchand Lalbhai Jain Pustakodhar Fund, Surat.

95 Dwâdashârnayachakra. Great work on Syâdwâda by Shri Mallavâdin. It is commented by Shri Yashovijayji.

100 Gnâtâdharmakathâ. 6th Anga Sutra. It has been commented by Shri Abaydeva suri. It deals with the lives of religious personages. Published in Babu Dhanpatsingji series, Calcutta.

100 Kalpa-Sutra. It deals with the lives of Mahavir, Parsvanath, Aristnemi, and Risobhnath. Translated in the Sacred Books of the East series vol. XXII. The author is shri Bhadrabâhuswâmi : there are many commentaries: The prevailing one is that of Shri Vinayvijayji, known as Sukhbodhika.

187 Kalpa. One of the chhed Sutras. There is a Niryukti on it by shri Bhadrabahuswâmi. It deals with special rules for Sâdhus. There is also a Bhâsya on it by Shri Sanghadasgani Mahattara: Commentator is Shri *K*shemakirti.

94 Karma-Granthas. It is a work on Karma-philosophy of the Jains. Six different

works viz. Karma-vipâk, Karma-Stava, Bandha-swâmitwa, Shadshiti, Satak, Saptatikâ,—come under this heading. Shri Shivsharma Suri is the author of old Satak and Shri Chandra Mahattarâcharya of Saptatikâ. Shri Malladhâri Hemchandrasuri and Shri Malaygiriji are the commentators on old Satak and Saptatikâ respectively. There are also old Karma Granthas and new ones. Authors of the old ones are different, and of the new five is Shri Devendra-Suri, and the same is the commentator on them. Four of the old ones are published by Shri Atmanand Jain Sabha (Bhaonagar), and five new ones with Saptatikâ by Shri Jain Dharma Prasarak Sabha (Bhaonagar). Old Satak is not yet published.

94 Karma-Prakriti—It deals with higher principles of Karma philosophy. Shri Shivsharma Suri is the author. He has extracted it from Agrayaniya Purva of Dristivâda Anga. There are two commentaries – one by Shri Malaygiriji and the other by Shri Yashovijayji. Both of them

are published—one by Devchand Lalbhai Jain Pustakodhar Fund, Surat, and the other by Shri Jain Dharma Prasarak sabha, Bhaonagar.

96 Nandisutra.—2nd Chulikâ Sutra : Author is Shri Devavâchakgani : and the commentator is Shri Malaygiriji. There is also a commentary on it by Shri Haribhadrasuri. The commentary of shri Malaygiriji with the text is published by Agamodaya Samiti, Surat. Shri Malaygiriji writes that his commentary is based on an old one by Shri Haribhadrasuri.

154 Niryâvalik—one of the Upângas.

187 Nishith—One of the chheda Sutras.

96 Nayayavatar—A work on logic by shri Siddhasena Divâker : It is commented by Shri Siddharshigani. Published by Shri Hemchandacharya Jain Sabha, Pâtan. Translated also into English by Dr. Satischandra Vidyabhusan Ph. D. Calcutta.

94 Panchasangraha—Standard work on Karma philosophy by Shri Chandra Mahattaracharya and commented by Shri Malaygiriji. Published by Hiralal Hansraja, Jamnagar.

96 Praman-Mimânsâ—Work on logic and philosophy in Sutra-style by Shri Hemchandrasuri. Commentary also has been written by him. Some portion is obtainable now : this is published by Sheth Mansukhbhai Bhagubhai, Ahmedabad.

96 Premeya-Kamal-Mârtand—commentary on Parikshâ-Mukh Sutras of shri Manikyanandi, by shri Prabhachandra-suri. To be had at Hindi Grantha Karyelaya, Bombay.

96 Praman-Samucchaya—a logical compendium of a Buddhist Acharya Dignâg. Shri Haribhadrasuri has commented on it.

96 Pragnâpanâ—4th Upânga. The author is Arya Syamâchârya. It is commented by shri Malaygiriji. Published by Agamodaya Samiti, Surat. Shri Malaygiri notes that his commentary is based on an old one by Shri Haribhadra Suri.

95 Sammatitarka—Work by Shri Siddhasena Divaker in Prakrit. It is a standard work on Jain philosophy. It is com mented by Rajgacchiya Abhayadevsuri. One part is published in Shri Yashovijaygi Grantha mala Bhavanagar.

94 Satak—Known as the 5th Karma Grantha. The author is shri Shivasarma Suri and commentator Shri Malyagiriji.

96 ShâstraVârtâSamucchya—The author is Shri Haribhadra Suri. It deals with all systems of philosophy. He himself has commented it. Another commentary known as Syâdyâdkalpalatâ is written by shri Yashovijayji. Published by shri Devchand Lalbhai Jain Pustakodhar Fund, Surat.

96 Shad-darsan-Samucchaya—Dealing with six systems of philosophy viz-Buddha, Nyâya, Sânkya, Jaina, Mimânsâ, and Chârvâka, The author is shri Haribhadrasuri; commentator is shri Gunaratnasuri. Published in Bibliothica Indica Series Calcutta.

96 Sutra-kritanga-2nd Anga sutra. Shri Bhadra bâhuswâmi has written a Niryukti on it. This Niryukti with the sutra is commented by shri Shilângâcharya. Published by Agamodaya Samiti, surat. Translated in the Sacred Books of the East series vol. XLV.

96 Syâdvâd-Manjari. It is a commentary by Mallisenasuri on Anya-yoga-Vyavachhedika of shri Hemchandrasuri. Published in shri Yashovijaya-Grantha-Mala, Series Bhaonagar.

95 Syâdvâd-Ratnâker—A great work of Shri Vadidevasuri, a contemporary of Shri Hemchandracharya. It is a commentary on Pramân-naya-tatwa-lokâlankâr, Sutras by him. Some portion of this great work is published by Sheth Mansukhbhai Bhagubhai, Ahmedabad.

96 Syâdvâd-rantâvtârikâ—Commentary on Pramâna-naya-tatwa lokâlankâr, by shri Ratnaprabhasuri. It is only a beginning to enter into a great work-Syâdvâdratnâker. Published by shri Yashovijayaji Granth-Mala Series Bhaonagar.

96 Tattvârtha—Work in Sutra Style. The Acharyas of the Swetamber and Digamber sects have written many commentaries on this work. The author is shri Umaswati. There is also a Bhâsya by the author himself. The principal commentators are Shri Siddhasengani, Shri Pujyapad-swami and Shri Akalankdeva.

173 Trishasti-salâkâ-purusha-charita-Historical work dealing with lives of 63 personages, written by shri Hemchandrâcharya. Published by shri Jain Dharma prasarak-sabha, Bhaonagar.

119 Visheshavâsyaka-bhâsya—It is a large commentary in Prakrit by shri Jinbhadragani Kshamâshraman, on the Niryukti of the Samâyik adyâya of the Avâsyaka Sutra. This Prakrit commentary is further commented by Maldhari Hemchandrasuri. It is also known as Sabdâmbhonidhi-Mahâbhâsyâ. Published in shri Yashovijayiji-Granthamala Series—Bhaonagar.

103 Yoniprabhrit—Author is Dharsena : it treats of different sciences.

ERRATA.

P.	L.	Incorrect.	Correct.
11	18	Perfom	Perform
13	10	Chundra	Chandra
18	22	donot	do not
20	12	are; God	are God.
31	7	Second	second
32	9	discrect	discreet
33	3	body excellent, form	body, excellent form
37	17	actions therefore	actions ; therefore
38	4	ad-infinitnm	ad-infinitum
38	15	unreal. Nothing	unreal, nothing
40	3	advaitism	Advaitism.
42	15	Prapanchor	Prapanch
44	8	madman	mad man
49	4	ever lasting	ever-lasting
50	14	pr. fix	prefix
51		sky flowers	sky-flowers.
53	11	rope	rope (see note on page 54.
56	6	kinds of	kinds of eternal substances.
56	12	eteanal	eternal.
59	5	God.	God

P.	L.	Incorrect.	Correct.
60	22	Grass	grass
60	25	ofGod	of God
62	18	nuinference	an inference.
63	4	God-just	God just
64	5	Form	From
64	13	up on	upon
66	7	towardse vil	towards evil
67	11	theyper form	they perform
69	11	theif	thief
76	7	positionis	position is
76	12	all-intelligent. Being	all-intelligent Being
78	9	swaım	swarm
82	4	O Mahadeo	" O Mahadeo
82	7	all	all "
84	4	prov	prove
86	13	man	men
88	14	water	(3) water
89	16	ambryo	embryo
92	6	dislike, senti-ments	dislike sentiments
94	9	deversions	divisions
95	21	Dwâdashasâr	Dwâdashâr
95	22	द्वादशसार	द्वादशार
96	2	स्रमुच्चय	समुच्चय
96	11	गंधास्ती	गंधहस्ति

P.	L.	Incorrect.	Correct.
96	16	Pramey	Praman
„	„	प्रमेय	प्रमाण
„	22	न्यायबतार	न्यायावतार
„	25	ष ड्	षट्
103	9	streng	strength
104	7	Concommittant	concomitant
„	8	inter	inner
106	5	self-existence	self-existent
111	15	extra ordinary	extraordinary
111	16	bind.	bind him.
114	4	well polished	well-polished
„	18	devine	divine
„	22	immemorable	immemorial
117	17	have estinguished	have been estinguish-ed.
123	17-18 *viz* I see,	a single form. and I do.	a single form *viz* I see and I do.
125	15	existance	existence
136	11	Concommitant	Concomitant
„	„	couse	cause
138	21	Christian	Christians
144	1	Dharma	Dharmi
„	15	can not	cannot
145	10	Dharmi	Dharma
152	11	red hot	red-hot
153	21	(*Shudhi-shâstra*).	*Shudhi-shâstra*.

P.	L.	Incorrect.	Correct
172	21	Curses	curses
175	13	Mahavir Lord	Lord Mahavir
176	22	$\frac{jn\hat{a}na}{he}$)	*jnana*)
179	15	Hstipala	Hastipala
112	19	can not	cannot
187	19	purificar tory	purificatory